MW00712124

LATIN

for Christian Schools®

ACTIVITIES MANUAL

TEACHER'S EDITION

Edith E. Smith

BJU Press
Greenville, South Carolina

NOTE:
The fact that materials produced by other publishers may be referred to in this volume does not constitute an endorsement by Bob Jones University Press of the content or theological position of materials produced by such publishers. The position of Bob Jones University Press, and the University itself, is well known. Any references and ancillary materials are listed as an aid to the student or the teacher and in an attempt to maintain the accepted academic standards of the publishing industry.

Latin Activities Manual for Christian Schools® Teacher's Edition

Edith E. Smith, M.A.

Editor
 Doug Rumminger

Compositor
 Nancy Lohr

for Christian Schools is a registered
trademark of Bob Jones University Press.

© 1999 Bob Jones University Press
Greenville, South Carolina 29614

Printed in the United States of America
All rights reserved

ISBN 1-57924-257-X

15   14   13   12   11   10   9   8   7   6

To the Student

Each activity is designed (1) to give you an opportunity to put into practice what you have just been taught and (2) to help you discover what you need to understand better. Study again any items that you answered incorrectly because all the future chapters are based on an understanding of the information of their preceding chapters.

As you write Latin phrases and sentences, say them aloud or, in the classroom, think how the words sound and what they mean.

Careful work on the activities will result in successful midterm and final examinations. More importantly, this work will give you an understanding of the Latin language that will be valuable to you throughout your life.

To the Teacher

The activities focus primarily on the material that immediately precedes their assignment. Of course, they are cumulative in the sense that they assume an understanding of the material presented previously.

As stated in the Teacher's Edition of the student text, each activity must be assigned exactly where it is cited in the student text. It should be checked then. The student can check his own work as you give the correct answers, or you can check the activities as homework. He needs to know and understand the right answers in order to progress successfully.

You should assign grades to about half of the activities in each chapter. No activities should be unassigned.

CAPITULUM I

You build your knowledge of Latin "block by block." The first chapters are as important as the foundation blocks of a house. If the foundation is firm, you can build on it with confidence.

Work all the way through each activity, answering all the questions the best you can. When you have finished, look for any items that you were unsure about. You can find the essential terms in bold type or in the titles of section headings in your text.

If you have to look for more than two or three answers, you should take time to study carefully the information in that section. Follow this procedure for each activity throughout the book.

Activity A

For each numbered item, write in the blank the matching meaning or definition from the list.

article	stilus	ille	quid	hic
meus	tuus	-t	liber	-ne

1. "your" _____ *tuus*

2. "what" _____ *quid*

3. "pen" _____ *stilus*

4. the enclitic that means "Here comes a question" _____ *-ne*

5. "this" (something near) _____ *hic*

6. "book" _____ *liber*

7. "my" _____ *meus*

8. "that" (something far) _____ *ille*

9. a kind of word not found in Latin _____ *article*

10. a verb ending _____ *-t*

© 1999 BJU Press. Reproduction prohibited.

Complete each sentence by filling in the blank.

1. To make a Latin vowel long, we place a _____*macron*_____ above it.

2. We have an idea how most Latin sounds were made because the letters have

   the same or similar sounds in the _____*Romance*_____ languages.

3. The last syllable of a Latin word is called the _____*ultima*_____.

4. The next-to-last syllable of a Latin word is called the _____*penult*_____.

5. Every syllable must contain a _____*vowel*_____.

6. There are _____*no*_____ silent letters in Latin.

If the word is correctly accented, write **Y** (for "yes") in the blank. If it is incorrectly accented, write the letter for the rule that should be applied.

Rules

        A. Never accent the ultima.

        B. Accent the penult if it is long.

___*Y*___ 1. lin′gua

___*A*___ 2. scholīs′

___*A*___ 3. liber′

___*Y*___ 4. Christiā′nīs

___*Y*___ 5. tu′us

© 1999 BJU Press. Reproduction prohibited.

Write the English meaning of each phrase and sentence without looking back in the chapter. Just trust your memory. When you complete the activity, check the chapter material to make any needed corrections. Draw a line through any incorrect words you may have and write the correct words after or above them.

1. liber meus ⎯⎯⎯⎯⎯ *my book* ⎯⎯⎯⎯⎯

2. lingua tua ⎯⎯⎯⎯⎯ *your language* ⎯⎯⎯⎯⎯

3. stilus tuus ⎯⎯⎯⎯⎯ *your pen* ⎯⎯⎯⎯⎯

Write the English meaning of sentences 4-7.

4. Hic est liber scholīs Latīnīs.

⎯⎯⎯⎯⎯⎯⎯⎯ *This is a book for Latin schools.* ⎯⎯⎯⎯⎯⎯⎯⎯

5. Ille est liber scholīs Christiānīs.

⎯⎯⎯⎯⎯⎯⎯⎯ *That is a book for Christian schools.* ⎯⎯⎯⎯⎯⎯⎯⎯

6. Ille est stilus meus.

⎯⎯⎯⎯⎯⎯⎯⎯ *That is my pen.* ⎯⎯⎯⎯⎯⎯⎯⎯

7. Hic est stilus tuus.

⎯⎯⎯⎯⎯⎯⎯⎯ *This is your pen.* ⎯⎯⎯⎯⎯⎯⎯⎯

Answer the questions in Latin, basing your answers on numbers 6 and 7.

8. Quid est ille?

⎯⎯⎯⎯⎯⎯⎯⎯ *Est stilus meus. / Ille est stilus meus.* ⎯⎯⎯⎯⎯⎯⎯⎯

9. Quid est hic?

⎯⎯⎯⎯⎯⎯⎯⎯ *Est stilus tuus. / Hic est stilus tuus.* ⎯⎯⎯⎯⎯⎯⎯⎯

© 1999 BJU Press. Reproduction prohibited.

Write the Latin word for each of these English words. Again, do not check the chapter material until you complete the activity. To make corrections, cross out your errors and write the correct answers after your first tries.

1. pen _____ *stilus* _____

2. book _____ *liber* _____

3. schools _____ *scholīs* _____

4. this _____ *hic* _____

5. that _____ *ille* _____

6. your _____ *tuus* _____

7. my _____ *meus* _____

This activity reviews the Essential Information in this chapter. Write *T* or *F* to indicate whether the statement is true or false.

___*T*___ 1. The noun *Rome* sometimes means a city in Italy and sometimes the whole Roman Empire.

___*F*___ 2. The word *Latium* is another term for the whole Roman Empire.

___*T*___ 3. In the title of this book, the endings -*a* and -*īs* are called *inflections*.

___*T*___ 4. Inflections show how words are used in sentences.

___*F*___ 5. The inflections of a noun and the adjective that modifies it must always be spelled the same.

___*T*___ 6. The enclitic -*ne* attached to the end of the first word of a Latin sentence tells the reader that what follows is a question.

© 1999 BJU Press. Reproduction prohibited.

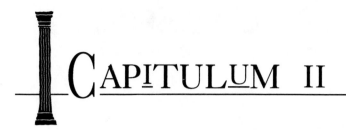

CAPITULUM II

© 1999 BJU Press. Reproduction prohibited.

Activity A

In each blank, write the word(s) from the list on page 14 that you think makes the most logical sentence.

Be prepared to read each sentence aloud in Latin and to tell what it means. Supply the articles *a, an,* or *the.* You can figure out the meaning of *Rōmānus* in sentence 8.
(Accept *a* for *the* and *the* for *a.*)

1. Marcus est _____*puer*_____ .
   (Marcus is a boy.)

2. Puer canem _____*(any verb listed)*_____ .
   (The boy [feeds] the dog.)

3. Mūs _____*fēlem*_____ timet.
   (The mouse fears the cat.)

4. Fēles _____*mūrem*_____ capit.
   (The cat catches a mouse.)

5. Quis equum _____*(any verb listed)*_____ ?
   (Who [has] a horse?)

6. _____*Puer*_____ equum habet.
   (The boy has a horse.)

7. Timetne equus mūrem? Equus mūrem _____*nōn timet*_____ .
   (Does the horse fear a mouse? The horse does not fear a mouse.)

8. Estne Marcus puer Rōmānus? Marcus est _____*puer Rōmānus*_____ .
   (Is Marcus a Roman boy? Marcus is a Roman boy.)

Activity B

Translate sentences 1-8, supplying articles and adjusting word order when necessary. Then answer questions 9 and 10.

1. Hic est canis. _____ *This is a dog.* _____
2. Ille est equus. _____ *That is a horse.* _____
3. Mūs fēlem timet. _____ *The mouse fears the cat.* _____
4. Fēles mūrem capit. _____ *The cat catches the mouse.* _____
5. Puer stilum habet. _____ *The boy has a pen/stylus.* _____
6. Antōnius Marcum docet. _____ *Antony/Anthony teaches Mark.* _____
7. Rōma° est urbs°. _____ *Rome is a city.* _____
   [°Rome; °city]
8. Quintus Rōmam dēfendit. _____ *Quintus defends Rome.* _____
9. Which sentences in this activity have linking verbs? _____ *1, 2, 7* _____
10. Which sentences have direct objects? _____ *3, 4, 5, 6, 8* _____

Activity C

In each blank write the letter of the item that matches the term.

_**H**___ 1. ultima   _**F**___ 6. predicate noun

_**G**___ 2. penult   _**B**___ 7. enclitic

_**I**___ 3. antepenult   _**A**___ 8. inflection

_**D**___ 4. linking verb   _**C**___ 9. macron

_**E**___ 5. direct object

A. word part that shows the grammatical use of a word

B. *-ne*, interrogative form attached to first word to show that a question is being asked

C. mark to distinguish a long vowel from a short vowel

D. word that is followed by a predicate noun

E. receiver of the action of a transitive verb

F. word that renames the subject

G. next-to-last syllable of a word

H. last syllable of a word

I. syllable that is accented if the penult is not long

© 1999 BJU Press. Reproduction prohibited.

Activity D

Fill in the blank(s) in the statement that follows each word.

1. *invenit*—The syllable that is accented is called the ___antepenult___.
This syllable is accented because the penult is short. **(in'venit)**

2. *canis*—The syllable called the ___penult___ is accented because
the syllable called the ___ultima___ cannot be accented. **(ca'nis)**

3. *Germāna*—The ___penult___ is long because it contains a
___long vowel___. **(Germā'na)**

4. *mūrem*—The ___penult___ is accented for two reasons: it
contains a ___long vowel___ and the ___ultima___ cannot
be accented. **(mū'rem)**

5. *dīligit*—The ___antepenult___ is accented because the
___penult___ is short. **(dī'ligit)**

Activity E

Translate sentences 1-5, supplying the subject when necessary. Then answer questions 6 and 7.

1. Marcus patriam° dīligit°. ___
Marcus loves the native land.
[°native land, country; °loves]

2. Patriam dēfendit. ___
He defends the country.

3. Quintus linguam Latīnam discit. ___
Quintus learns the Latin language.

4. Magister linguam Anglicam docet. ___
The teacher teaches the English language.

5. Linguam Germānam nōn dīcit. ___
He/She does not speak the German language.

6. Which sentences in this activity do not have a noun subject? ___
2, 5

7. Are the verbs in this activity transitive active or linking? ___
transitive active

This activity reviews the pronunciation rules found in Chapters 1 and 2. Fill in the blanks with the correct information.

1. Rules for dividing a word into syllables

   a. Be sure that each syllable contains a _____*vowel*_____.

   b. If two vowels are together, divide _____*between them*_____.

   c. A single consonant between two vowels goes with the vowel that

      _____*follows it*_____.

   d. Two consonants that form a blend (are/are not) _____*are*_____

      in the same syllable.

   e. If two consonants do not form a blend, divide _____*between them*_____.

2. Rules for accenting a word

   a. Never accent the _____*ultima*_____.

   b. Accent the penult if it is _____*long*_____.

      The penult is long if it contains a vowel that is _____*long*_____.

      The penult is long if it ends with a _____*consonant*_____.

   c. If the penult is not accented, the accent must be on the

      _____*antepenult / syllable before the penult*_____.

© 1999 BJU Press. Reproduction prohibited.

A. Label each subject *S,* each linking verb *LV,* and each transitive active verb *TrV.* (Remember that when the subject in Latin is omitted, the verb inflection implies the subject. Since we need the subject in an English sentence, you may use *this, that, he, she,* or *it* in your translations.)

B. If the sentence has a predicate noun, label that word *PN;* if it has a direct object, label that *DO.* Do not label adjectives.

C. Write the translation.

           S   **DO**   **TrV**
1. Marcus patriam dēfendit. _____ *Marcus defends the country.* _____

           DO   **S**   **TrV**
2. Patriam Marcus dēfendit. _____ *Marcus defends the country.* _____

           DO   **TrV**
3. Patriam dīligit. _____ *He loves the country.* _____

              DO   **TrV**
4. Linguam Anglicam dīcit. _____ *He speaks the English language.* _____

           S   **LV** **PN**
5. Rōma est urbs. _____ *Rome is a city.* _____

           S   **LV** **PN**
6. Quintus est puer Rōmānus. _____ *Quintus is a Roman boy.* _____

D. Answer these questions.

1. What predicate noun(s) do you find in the sentences above? ____ *urbs, puer* ____

2. What direct object(s) do you find? _____ *patriam, Patriam, Patriam, Linguam* ____

3. From sentences 1 and 2, what do you notice about word order in Latin?

                                    It can vary.

4. What transitive active verbs are in the sentences? _____

                    dēfendit, dēfendit, dīligit, dīcit

© 1999 BJU Press. Reproduction prohibited.

Answer these questions in complete Latin sentences. Remember that Latin word order can differ from English word order. Generally, transitive active verbs come at the end of the sentence and subjects come at the beginning of the sentence. Variations from these general rules are for the purpose of emphasis. Also remember that a noun subject may be omitted if it is understood from a previous sentence. Context can help you recall the meanings of the words.

1. Marcus stilum habet. Habetne Marcus stilum? _____

   _____*Marcus stilum habet.*_____

   (Marcus has a stylus. Does Marcus have a stylus?)

2. Stilum invenit. Quis stilum invenit? _____

   _____*Marcus stilum invenit.*_____

   (He finds the stylus. Who finds the stylus?)

3. Marcus linguam Latīnam discit. Quid Marcus discit? _____

   _____*Linguam Latīnam Marcus discit.*_____

   (Marcus learns the Latin language. What does Marcus learn?)

4. Quis linguam Latīnam discit? _____

   _____*Marcus linguam Latīnam discit.*_____

   (Who learns the Latin language?)

5. Mūrem Quintus capit. Capitne Quintus mūrem? _____

   _____*Quintus mūrem capit.*_____

   (Quintus catches the mouse. Does Quintus catch the mouse?)

6. Rōma nōn est urbs mea. Estne urbs tua? _____

   _____*Nōn est urbs mea. / Est urbs mea.*_____

   (Rome is not my city. Is it your city?)

© 1999 BJU Press. Reproduction prohibited.

Without looking at the word lists, write the English meaning of each Latin word. Then check your answers with the word lists and take time *now* to learn the meaning of any that you left blank or for which you gave the wrong meaning.

1. canis _____ dog _____
2. equus _____ horse _____
3. hic _____ this _____
4. ille _____ that _____
5. liber _____ book _____
6. patria _____ native land / country _____
7. porcus _____ pig _____
8. truncus _____ tree trunk _____
9. tuus _____ your _____
10. urbs _____ city _____
11. meus _____ my _____
12. quis _____ who? _____
13. quid _____ what? _____
14. capit _____ catches _____
15. dēfendit _____ defends _____
16. dīcit _____ says _____
17. dīligit _____ loves _____
18. discit _____ learns _____
19. habet _____ has _____

© 1999 BJU Press. Reproduction prohibited.

CAPITULUM III

Activity A

For each question you are given two possible answers. They are connected by the conjunction *aut,* meaning "or." Write the correct noun choice in the blank.

1. Quis est puer, discipula aut discipulus? _____ *discipulus* _____
   (Who is a boy, a female student or a male student?)

2. Quis est Quintus, magister aut magistra? _____ *magister* _____
   (Who is Quintus, a male teacher or a female teacher?)

3. Quis linguam Latīnam docet, discipula aut magistra? _____ *magistra* _____
   (Who teaches the Latin language, the student or the teacher?)

4. Quid magister habet, urbem aut librum? _____ *librum* _____
   (What does the teacher have, a city or a book?)

5. Quem magister docet, puerum aut Rōmam? _____ *puerum* _____
   (Whom does the teacher teach, the boy or Rome?)

6. Quis discipulam docet, patria aut magistra? _____ *magistra* _____
   (Who teaches the student, the country or the teacher?)

Activity B

Notice carefully how the words are marked, and then pronounce each word aloud. The letters in bold type emphasize the rules for syllable division.

1. scho′la
2. tu′us
3. ca′nis
4. Mar′cus
5. dis′cit
6. sanc′tus
7. lin′gua
8. ma gis′tra
9. Rō mā′nus
10. An′gli cam
11. pa′tri a

© 1999 BJU Press. Reproduction prohibited.

Answer these questions about the syllable division and the accents of the eleven words in Activity B.

1. In number 1, why is the syllable division after *scho* instead of *sch?* _____
   _____ *Each syllable must contain a vowel.* _____

2. What makes the penult long in number 7? _____
   _____ *It ends with a consonant.* _____

3. What makes the penult long in number 9? _____
   _____ *There is a long vowel in the penult.* _____

4. Why are numbers 1-3 accented on the penult? _____
   _____ *The ultima cannot be accented.* _____

5. What is the name of the syllable that is accented in numbers 10-11? ___*antepenult*___

6. Why is the penult not accented in number 11? _____
   _____ *It does not contain a long vowel, and it does not end with a consonant.* _____

© 1999 BJU Press. Reproduction prohibited.

Copy the words. Draw a vertical line between the syllables and mark the accent in each word. Be prepared to give the reason for each syllable division and each accent mark.

1. discipulus _____dis / ci′ / pu / lus_____ (Divide between consonants that do not blend; put a single consonant with the vowel that follows; same. Accent the antepenult if the penult is short.)

2. Ītalia _____Ī / ta′ / li / a_____ (Put a single consonant with the vowel that follows it; same; divide between vowels. Accent the antepenult if the penult is short.)

3. dēfendit _____dē / fen′ / dit_____ (Put a single consonant with the vowel that follows it; divide between consonants unless they form a blend. Accent the penult if it is long.)

4. amīcus _____a / mī′ / cus_____ (Put a single consonant with the vowel that follows it; same. Accent the penult if it is long.)

5. compendium _____com / pen′ / di / um_____ (Divide between consonants unless they form a blend; same; divide between vowels. Accent the antepenult if the penult is short.)

6. Deus _____De′ / us_____ (Divide between vowels. Do not accent the ultima.)

In each blank write the correct form from the choices given.

1. Discipulus _____stilum_____ (stilus, stilum) habet.
   (The [male] pupil has a stylus.)

2. Quoque° _____librum_____ (librum, liber) habet.
   [°also] **(He also has a book.)**

3. Magistra _____discipulum_____ (discipulum, discipulus) docet.
   (The [female] teacher teaches the [male] pupil.)

4. Amīcus meus _____urbem_____ (urbem, urbs) dīligit.
   (My friend loves the city.)

5. Quoque° _____patriam_____ (patria, patriam) dīligit.
   [°also] **(He also loves the country.)**

6. _____Linguam meam_____ (Lingua mea, Linguam meam) dīcit.
   (He speaks my language.)

7. _____Quis_____ (Quis, Quem) linguam Latīnam discit?
   (Who learns the Latin language?)

8. _____Quem_____ (Quis, Quem) magistra docet?
   (Whom does the [female] teacher teach?)

© 1999 BJU Press. Reproduction prohibited.

Write each sentence in Latin, being careful to put a macron over each long vowel. (Only two macrons are needed for the entire activity.) Be prepared to read your Latin sentences aloud.

1. Marcus is a pupil. _____
   _____ *Marcus est discipulus.* _____

2. The teacher teaches the Latin language. _____
   _____ *Magister/Magistra linguam Latīnam docet.* _____

3. Who has a book? _____
   _____ *Quis librum habet?* _____

4. Does Marcus have a pen? _____
   _____ *Habetne Marcus stilum?* _____

5. Cornelia is a pupil. _____
   _____ *Cornēlia est discipula.* _____

Read these sentences and answer in Latin the questions that follow. In some of the answers, you will need to use the adjective *meus*.

Hic est canis meus. Canis meus lupum nōn timet.

Habet magister meus equum. Equum docet. Cornēlius est amīcus meus. Equum quoque [also] habet. Capit et pascit equum.

1. Estne hic canis tuus? _____
   _____ *Hic canis est meus. / Hic est canis meus.* _____

2. Timetne canis tuus lupum? _____
   _____ *Canis meus lupum nōn timet.* _____

3. Quid magister tuus habet? _____
   _____ *Equum magister meus habet. / Magister meus equum habet. / Equum habet.* _____

4. Quis equum docet? _____
   _____ *Magister meus equum docet. / Equum magister meus docet.* _____

5. Quis est amīcus tuus? _____
   _____ *Cornēlius est amīcus meus. / Amīcus meus est Cornēlius.* _____

6. Quis equum capit et pascit? _____
   _____ *Cornēlius equum capit et pascit.* _____

© 1999 BJU Press. Reproduction prohibited.

Write each sentence in English. Remember that word order in Latin does not determine the function of a word; word inflections determine whether a word is a subject or a direct object.

1. Gregem° pastor dūcit°. _____ *The pastor/shepherd leads the flock.* _____
   [°flock; °leads]

2. Grex° pastōrem dīligit. _____ *The flock loves the pastor/shepherd.* _____
   [°flock]

3. Puerum pater° dūcit. _____ *The father leads the boy.* _____
   [°father]

4. Puer canem dūcit. _____ *The boy leads the dog.* _____

5. Pater puerum dīligit. _____ *The father loves the boy.* _____

6. Puer patrem dīligit. _____ *The boy loves the father.* _____

Answer the following questions.

1. What is the origin of the word *Romance?* _____ *Roman/Rome* _____

2. What six languages are called Romance languages? _____
   French, Spanish, Italian, Portuguese, Romanian, and Romansch

3. When did the Romans first invade Britain? _____ *54 B.C.* _____

4. When did the Angles and Saxons first invade Britain? _____ *A.D. 449* _____

5. When did the Norman French first invade England? _____ *A.D. 1066* _____

6. From which invaders did the island get the name *England?* _____ *the Angles* _____

7. From which invaders did place-names in England such as *Chester* and *Lancaster* come? _____ *the Romans* _____

8. From which invaders did a large number of words with Latin origin come? _____
   the Normans/French

9. What is the meaning of B.C.? _____ *before (the birth of) Christ* _____

10. What is the meaning of A.D. (anno Domini)? _____ *in the year of the Lord* _____

11. English is not a Romance language. What kind of language is it? _____ *Germanic* _____

© 1999 BJU Press. Reproduction prohibited.

Follow the directions for each section. Complete the activity without looking at Chapter 2. Then use the book to correct (with a different colored pencil or ink) any errors you may have made.

1. Write the accusative form and the meaning of each word.

   a. mūs _____ *mūrem, mouse* _____

   b. amīcus _____ *amīcum, friend* _____

   c. quis _____ *quem, who/whom* _____

   d. puer _____ *puerum, child/boy* _____

   e. magistra _____ *magistram, (female) teacher* _____

   f. urbs _____ *urbem, city* _____

   g. canis _____ *canem, dog* _____

2. Give the meaning and the part of speech of each word.

   a. nōn _____ *not, adverb* _____

   b. dūcit _____ *leads, verb* _____

   c. quoque _____ *also, adverb* _____

   d. aut _____ *or, conjunction* _____

   e. quis _____ *who, pronoun / interrogative pronoun* _____

© 1999 BJU Press. Reproduction prohibited.

Seeing words in sentences will help you remember the word meanings. This vocabulary review includes all the new words in this chapter and a few review words from Chapter 1. Write the sentences in English. For teachers and pupils, say "man teacher, woman teacher, boy student, girl student."

1. Magister docet. _____ *The man teacher teaches.* _____

2. Magistra quoque docet. _____ *The woman teacher also teaches.* _____

3. Discipula discit. _____ *The girl student learns.* _____

4. Discipulus quoque discit. _____ *The boy student also learns.* _____

5. Quis est amīcus tuus? _____ *Who is your friend?* _____

6. Mūs lupum timet. _____ *The mouse fears the wolf.* _____

7. Ille est Cornēlius. _____ *That is Cornelius.* _____

8. Cornēlius Deum dīligit. _____ *Cornelius loves God.* _____

9. Estne Ītalia patria tua? _____ *Is Italy your country?* _____

10. Cornēlius canem habet. _____ *Cornelius has a dog.* _____

11. Quintus equum habet. _____ *Quintus has a horse.* _____

12. Quid Marcus habet? _____ *What does Marcus have?* _____

© 1999 BJU Press. Reproduction prohibited.

CAPITULUM IV

Write each of these words in the genitive case.

1. discipula _____ *discipulae* _____
2. discipulus _____ *discipulī* _____
3. diēs _____ *diēī* _____
4. manus _____ *manūs* _____
5. schola _____ *scholae* _____
6. canis _____ *canis* _____
7. equus _____ *equī* _____
8. urbs _____ *urbis* _____
9. liber _____ *librī* _____
10. mūs _____ *mūris* _____

Activity B

Write each sentence in Latin.

1. Mark has a dog. _____
   Marcus canem habet. _____

2. The dog's name is Lucius. _____
   Nōmen canis est Lucius. _____

3. Quintus is Mark's friend. _____
   Quintus est amīcus Marcī. _____

4. Antony is a pupil of Secundus. _____
   Antōnius est discipulus Secundī. _____

5. Secundus is Antony's teacher. _____
   Secundus est magister Antoniī/Antōnī. _____

6. Mark is a friend of the king. _____
   Marcus est amīcus rēgis. _____

© 1999 BJU Press. Reproduction prohibited.

7. Who is the leader [princeps] of the senate? _____

   _____ *Quis est princeps senātūs?* _____

8. What is the name of the country? _____

   _____ *Quid est nōmen patriae?* _____

Activity C

Write each sentence in Latin.

1. Quintus is the son of the conqueror. _____

   _____ *Quintus est fīlius victōris.* _____

2. Mark is a teacher of language. _____

   _____ *Marcus est magister linguae.* _____

3. What is Cornelius's country? _____

   _____ *Quid est patria Cornēlī/Cornēliī?* _____

4. Who is the king of the country? _____

   _____ *Quis est rēx patriae?* _____

5. Does the king defend the country? _____

   _____ *Dēfenditne rēx patriam?* _____

Activity D

Write the following phrases in Latin. If you need help, refer to pages 46-51, where the declensions and the genitive forms of nouns are given.

1. the language of the country _____ *lingua patriae* _____

2. a city of Italy _____ *urbs Ītaliae* _____

3. Quintus's book _____ *liber Quintī* _____

4. a friend of Quintus _____ *amīcus Quintī* _____

5. the life of the king _____ *vīta rēgis* _____

6. the king's friend _____ *amīcus rēgis* _____

7. the glory of the senate _____ *glōria senātūs* _____

8. the name [nōmen] of the day _____ *nōmen diēī* _____

© 1999 BJU Press. Reproduction prohibited.

Write these sentences in English.

1. Christus est Salvātor. _____ *Christ is the Savior.* _____

2. Est Fīlius Deī. _____ *He is the Son of God.* _____

3. Quoque° est amīcus peccātōris. _____ *Also He is the friend of a/the sinner. / He is also . . .* _____
   [°Also]

4. Viam vītae ostendit. _____ *He shows the way of life.* _____

5. Est Dominus et Rēx. _____ *He is Lord and King.* _____

6. Christiānus magnum Rēgem dīligit. _____ *The/A Christian loves the great King.* _____

7. Christiānus magnam spem habet. _____ *The/A Christian has great hope.* _____

Activity F

Answer these questions in complete Latin sentences.

1. Quintus equum habet. Cuius equus est ille? _____ *Ille est equus Quintī.* _____
   _____ **(Quintus has a horse. Whose horse is that?)**

2. Marcus librum habet. Cuius liber est ille? _____ *Ille est liber Marcī.* _____
   _____ **(Marcus has a book. Whose book is that?)**

3. Antōnius stilum habet. Cuius stilus est hic? _____ *Hic est stilus Antōnī/Antōniī.* _____
   _____ **(Antonius has a stylus. Whose stylus is this?)**

4. Tullius° est discipulus Secundī. Cuius magister est Secundus? _____ *Secundus est magister*
   _____ *Tullī/Tulliī.* **(Tullius is Secundus's pupil. / Tullius is a student of Secundus.**
   [°a person's name] **Whose teacher is Secundus?)**

5. Claudius° est fīlius magistrī. Cuius pater° est magister? _____ *Pater Claudī/Claudiī est*
   _____ *magister.* **(Claudius is the teacher's son. / Claudius is the son of the teacher.**
   [°a person's name; °father] **Whose father is the teacher?)**

© 1999 BJU Press. Reproduction prohibited.

This activity is based on the sentences in Activity E.

1. Divide the syllables and mark the accents in these words: *Fīliī*, *Fīlī*, and *viae*.

   Fī' / li / ī, Fī' / lī, vī' / ae

2. What nouns are modified by adjectives? _____ *Rēgem, spem* _____

3. What three nouns are modified by nouns in the genitive case?

   Fīlius, amīcus, viam

4. Which four sentences have implied subjects instead of a nominative noun or pronoun

   as the subject? _____ *2, 3, 4, 5* _____

5. Which three sentences contain direct objects? _____ *4, 6, 7* _____

6. Which four sentences contain predicate nouns? _____ *1, 2, 3, 5* _____

7. Which three third-declension nouns are used? (Give the nominative form of each.)

   Salvātor, peccātor, Rēx

8. What fifth-declension noun is used? _____ *spem* _____

9. Why does *magnum/magnam* precede the nouns it modifies in sentences 6 and 7?

   An adjective that precedes the noun it modifies receives special emphasis.

© 1999 BJU Press. Reproduction prohibited.

Follow the directions for each item.

1. Divide the words into syllables and mark the accents.

    patriae _____ *pa' / tri / ae* _____

    Fīliī _____ *Fī' / li / ī* _____

    Salvātōris _____ *Sal / vā / tō' / ris* _____

2. Give the English equivalent for the Latin letter *v*. _____ *w* _____

3. Give the stem of each word. At the end of each stem, put a hyphen.

    vīta, vītae _____ *vīt-* _____

    mūs, mūris _____ *mūr-* _____

    Antōnius, Antōniī, or Antōnī _____ *Antōni-* _____

    rēx, rēgis _____ *rēg-* _____

4. From the words in the first three parts of this activity, give a word that illustrates each of these items.

    a. the nominative form of an *i*-stem noun _____ *Antōnius* _____

    b. an elision _____ *Antōnī* _____

    c. a diphthong _____ *patriae/vītae* _____

© 1999 BJU Press. Reproduction prohibited.

Activity I

Answer these questions in Latin, basing your answers on the sentences in Activity E. Your answers should be complete sentences.

1. Quis est Christus? (A five-part answer is needed.) _____ *Christus est Salvātor, Fīlius Deī,*

   _____ *amīcus peccātōris, Dominus, et Rēx.* **(Who is Christ?)**

2. Quid Christus ostendit? _____ *Christus viam vītae ostendit.*

   _____ **(What does Christ show?)**

3. Quem Christiānus dīligit? _____ *Christiānus magnum Rēgem dīligit.*

   _____ **(Whom does a Christian love?)**

4. Cuius Fīlius est Christus? _____ *Christus est Fīlius Deī. / Est Fīlius Deī.*

   _____ **(Whose Son is Christ?)**

5. Cuius amīcus est Christus? _____ *Christus est amīcus peccātōris. / Est amīcus peccātōris.*

   _____ **(Whose friend is Christ?)**

Activity J

This vocabulary review covers words found in this chapter and in Chapters 1 and 2. For numbers 1-11, translate the noun phrases (nouns modified by adjectives, by interrogative adjectives, or by genitive case nouns). For numbers 12-15, write each sentence in English.

1. Fīlius Deī _____ *Son of God*

2. Dominus meus _____ *my Lord*

3. glōria magna _____ *great glory*

4. nōmen peccātōris _____ *name of the sinner*

5. via vītae _____ *way of life*

6. victor Rōmānus _____ *Roman conqueror*

7. senātus Rōmae _____ *senate of Rome / Rome's senate*

8. diēs nova _____ *new day*

9. cuius magister _____ *whose teacher / teacher of whom*

10. Salvātor et Rēx meus _____ *my Savior and King / the Savior and my King*

11. spēs peccātōris _____ *hope of the sinner*

12. Puer Rōmānus Ītaliam dīligit. _____ *The Roman boy loves Italy.*

13. Mūs canem timet. _____ *The mouse fears the dog.*

14. Hic est diēs speī. _____ *This is a day of hope.*

15. Salvātor viam vītae ostendit. _____ *The Savior shows the way of life.*

© 1999 BJU Press. Reproduction prohibited.

CAPITULUM V

© 1999 BJU Press. Reproduction prohibited.

Activity A

Try to answer the questions without looking at the chapter. Then check your answers with the chapter. Fill in any that you omitted, correct any that are wrong, and circle all of these. Reread the information concerning any answers you did not know and take time to learn these answers.

1. Give the meaning of these terms.

   a. pāx Rōmāna _____ Roman peace _____

   b. SPQR _____ The Roman Senate and People _____

   c. -que _____ and _____

2. Give the names requested.

   a. first Roman emperor _____ Augustus Caesar / Caesar Augustus _____

   b. a Roman military officer who accepted Christ _____ Cornelius/Cornēlius _____

   c. the man who completed the first Latin translation of the Bible _____ Jerome _____

Activity B

A. Read the eight sentences aloud.

B. Find the verses in the King James Version of the Gospel of John. In each verse find the words in which Christ says "I am." Figure out the meaning of the Latin words following *Ego sum*. In number 7, notice that the word *et* occurs twice.

C. Write the translation of each sentence.

1. Ego sum pānis vītae. (6:48) _____ I am the/that bread of life. _____

2. Ego sum pānis vīvus. (6:51) _____ I am the living bread. _____

3. Ego sum lūx mundī. (8:12) _____ I am the light of the world. _____

4. Ego sum ostium. (10:9) _____ I am the door. _____

5. Ego sum pastor bonus. (10:11) _____ I am the good shepherd. _____

Written exercises   **27**

6. Ego sum resurrectio et vīta. (11:25) _____ *I am the resurrection and the life.*

_____

7. Ego sum via et vēritās et vīta. (14:6) _____ *I am the way and the truth and the life.*

_____

8. Ego sum vītis vēra: et Pater meus agricola est. (15:1) _____ *I am the true vine,*

and my Father is the husbandman/farmer.

_____

Activity C

Complete each sentence from the Gospel of John by filling in the blank with the correct Latin word. After answering as many as you can from what you remember, use Activity B to correct and complete your work. Circle any answers that you changed or filled in and take time to learn those words.

1. _____ *Ego* _____ sum ostium.
   (I am the door.)

2. Ego sum pānis _____ *vīvus* _____.
   (I am the living bread.)

3. Ego sum lūx _____ *mundī* _____.
   (I am the light of the world.)

4. Ego sum resurrectio et _____ *vīta* _____.
   (I am the resurrection and the life.)

5. Ego sum _____ *pastor* _____ bonus.
   (I am the good shepherd.)

6. Ego sum via et _____ *vēritās* _____ et _____ *vīta* _____.
   (I am the way and the truth and the life.)

7. Ego sum _____ *vītis* _____ vēra.
   (I am the true vine.)

8. Pater meus _____ *agricola* _____ est.
   (My Father is the husbandman/farmer.)

© 1999 BJU Press. Reproduction prohibited.

© 1999 BJU Press. Reproduction prohibited.

Activity D

After each noun write the genitive form and the English meaning.

1. agricola _____agricolae_____   _____husbandman_____

2. lūx _____lūcis_____   _____light_____

3. mundus _____mundī_____   _____world_____

4. ostium _____ostiī/ostī_____   _____door_____

5. pānis _____pānis_____   _____bread_____

6. Pater _____Patris_____   _____Father (God)_____

7. resurrectio _____resurrectiōnis_____   _____resurrection_____

8. vēritās _____vēritātis_____   _____truth_____

9. vītis _____vītis_____   _____vine_____

After each word write the part of speech (adjective, pronoun, or verb) and the English meaning.

10. bonus _____adjective_____   _____good_____

11. vēra _____adjective_____   _____true_____

12. vīvus _____adjective_____   _____living_____

13. ego _____pronoun_____   _____I_____

14. sum _____verb_____   _____I am_____

Activity E

List all the noun phrases found in Activity B.

1. _____pānis vītae_____

2. _____pānis vīvus_____

3. _____lūx mundī_____

4. _____pastor bonus_____

5. _____vītis vēra_____

6. _____Pater meus_____

Written exercises

Activity F

Read aloud these verses from the Gospel of John and then translate them.

1. Pater dīligit Fīlium. (3:35) _____ *The Father loves the Son.* _____

2. Deus est Spiritus. (4:24) _____ *God is a Spirit.* _____

3. Hic est vērē Prophēta. (7:40) _____ *This is truly the prophet. / Truly this is the prophet.* _____

4. Quid est vēritās? (18:38) _____ *What is truth?* _____

Activity G

Answer each question in a complete Latin sentence.

1. Quis est Fīlius Deī? _____ *Christus est Fīlius Deī.* _____
   (Who is the Son of God?)

2. Quis Fīlium dīligit? _____ *Pater Fīlium dīligit.* _____
   (Who loves the Son?)

3. Quis est pānis vītae et vītis vēra? _____ *Christus est panis vītae et vītis vēra.* _____
   (Who is the bread of life and the true vine?)

4. Quis est agricola? _____ *Pater est agricola.* _____
   (Who is the husbandman/farmer?)

Activity H

Using the sentences in Activities B, F, and G, give the information requested.

1. Name the three nouns in the genitive case. _____ *vītae, mundī, Deī* _____

2. Name the four adjectives. _____ *vīvus, bonus, vēra, meus* _____

3. Give the activity letter and the sentence number of the sentences that have a transitive verb and a direct object. _____ *Activity F, number 1; Activity G, number 2* _____

4. Name the adverb. _____ *vērē* _____

5. Name the interrogative pronouns. _____ *quid, quis* _____

© 1999 BJU Press. Reproduction prohibited.

Label the case of each noun and pronoun in the following sentences (*not* the adjectives *magna* and *bonus*). Write one of these abbreviations over each noun or pronoun: N (nominative), G (genitive), A (accusative).

   1. Christus est Fīlius Deī. **(Christ is the Son of God.)**
       N   N   G

   2. Est Salvātor mundī. **(He is the Savior of the world.)**
          N   G

   3. Glōria Dominī est magna. **(The glory of the Lord is great.)**
       N   G

   4. Scriptūra est vēritās. **(Scripture is truth.)**
       N   N

   5. Christiānus bonus dīligit Dominum. **(A good Christian loves the Lord.)**
       N   A

   6. Ego sum Christiānus. **(I am a Christian.)**
       N   N

In the first blank write the Latin word that gives a clue to the meaning of the English word. For nouns write the genitive form. In the second blank write the English meaning of the Latin origin. Choose from the words you have worked with in Activities B, C, F, G, and I. For number 1 use the Latin adverb origin and for number 2 use the noun origin. Take time to learn any information you look up.

  1. verily   *vērē*   *truly*

  2. verity   *vēritātis*   *truth*

  3. filial   *fīlī/fīliī*   *son*

  4. deity   *Deī*   *God*

  5. egotistical   *ego*   *I*

  6. vital   *vītae*   *life*

  7. lucid   *lūcis*   *light*

  8. agriculture   *agricolae*   *farmer*

  9. viaduct   *viae*   *road/way*

10. mundane   *mundī*   *world*

11. population   *populī*   *people*

12. prophetic   *prophētae*   *prophet*

© 1999 BJU Press. Reproduction prohibited.

This vocabulary review covers words found in this chapter and words from Chapters 1-4. The contexts should help you remember the meanings. Write each phrase and sentence in English.

1. populus Rōmae _____ *the people of Rome / Rome's people*

2. verbum senātūs _____ *the word of the senate / the senate's word*

3. fīlius patris _____ *son of the father / the father's son*

4. spēs Christiānī _____ *hope of a Christian / the Christian's hope*

5. lūx mundī _____ *the light of the world*

6. pānis vītae _____ *the bread of life*

7. vītis vēra _____ *the true vine*

8. pānis vīvus _____ *the living bread*

9. prophēta Deī _____ *a prophet of God / God's prophet*

10. resurrectiō et vīta _____ *the resurrection and the life*

11. Spiritus Deī _____ *the Spirit of God*

12. Agricola equum habet. _____ *The farmer has a horse.*

13. Patria rēgem habet. _____ *The country has a king.*

14. Quis spem magnam habet? _____ *Who has great hope?*

© 1999 BJU Press. Reproduction prohibited.

CAPITULUM VI

© 1999 BJU Press. Reproduction prohibited.

Activity A

Fill in the blanks with the correct words or phrases.

1. The Vulgate is a translation of the Bible into the _____Latin_____ language.

2. The Latin scholar who produced the Vulgate was _____Jerome_____.

3. Besides *Vulgate,* another English derivative from the Latin word *vulgus* is

   _____vulgar_____, which comes from the meaning "mob" or "rabble."

4. A section of the Vulgate that is not accepted by non-Catholic churches as being

   inspired by God is called the _____Apocrypha_____.

5. During the Protestant Reformation in the sixteenth century, a friend of John Calvin,

   whose name was _____(Theodore) Beza_____, translated the New Testament and

   Psalms into Latin.

Activity B

Write each of the following words in the dative case. To determine the dative form, follow these steps. (1) Decide from the genitive form what declension each noun is. (2) Write its dative form from memory. (3) Check your answers with the list of case inflections for the five declensions. (4) Correct any errors you may have made.

1. victor, victōris _____victōrī_____

2. via, viae _____viae_____

3. senātus, senātūs _____senātuī_____

4. diēs, diēī _____diēī_____

5. Dominus, Dominī _____Dominō_____

6. agricola, agricolae _____agricolae_____

7. vēritās, vēritātis _____vēritātī_____

8. verbum, verbī _____verbō_____

9. lūx, lūcis _____lūcī_____

10. spēs, speī _____speī_____

Here are words in each declension. Write each word in the four cases. For *verbum*, the case forms are given for you because it involves a form that has not yet been explained. Remember the difference between *diēs* and *spēs* when writing the fifth-declension form. Practice saying aloud what you have written, giving the case name before each case form.

First declension: **grātia** _____ grātia, grātiae, grātiae, grātiam

Second declension: **agnus** _____ agnus, agnī, agnō, agnum

Second declension: **verbum** _____ verbum, verbī, verbō, verbum

Third declension: **rēx** _____ rēx, rēgis, rēgī, rēgem

Fourth declension: **quercus** _____ quercus, quercūs, quercuī, quercum

Fifth declension: **diēs** _____ diēs, diēī, diēī, diem

Activity D

Write each word in Latin, being careful to use the correct inflection for the function indicated. If you are unsure of the declension of any of these nouns, check the genitive forms in the Vocābulārium section of this book.

1. hope—subject _____ spēs

2. name—subject _____ nōmen

3. Rome—possessive _____ Rōmae

4. mouse—possessive _____ mūris

5. people—possessive _____ populī

6. oak tree—indirect object _____ quercuī

7. book—indirect object _____ librō

8. door—indirect object _____ ostiō

9. boy—direct object _____ puerum

10. resurrection—direct object _____ resurrectiōnem

© 1999 BJU Press. Reproduction prohibited.

© 1999 BJU Press. Reproduction prohibited.

Activity E

Translate these sentences. Each sentence contains at least one first- or fifth-declension noun in the genitive or dative case. Number 4 is not as hard as it may first appear.

1. Magistrae librum discipulus dedit. _____

   _____ *A pupil gave the teacher a book.* _____

2. Magistra Juliae librum ostendit. _____

   _____ *The teacher shows Julia the book.* _____

3. Amīcus Juliae librum legitº. _____ *Julia's friend is reading the book. /* _____

   _____ *A friend is reading the book to Julia. / A friend is reading Julia the book.* _____

   [ºreads, is reading]

4. Liber novus magistrae nostraeº patriae nostrae magnam glōriam dat. _____

   _____ *Our teacher's new book gives our country great glory.* _____

   [ºour]

5. Initiumº diēī novae est tempusº speī. _____

   _____ *The beginning of a new day is a time of/for hope.* _____

   [ºbeginning; ºtime]

Activity F

Above each underlined word write the abbreviation for the case of that noun or pronoun. Use these abbreviations.

N (nominative)	*D* (dative)
G (genitive)	*A* (accusative)

1.   **N**   **G** **D**   **A**
   <u>Verbum</u> <u>Deī</u> <u>mihi</u> <u>vēritātem</u> ostendit.

   (The Word of God shows me truth / shows truth to me.)

2.   **D**   **A**
   Christus <u>peccātōrī</u> <u>veniam</u> praebet.

   (Christ offers the sinner forgiveness.)

3.   **D**   **G**   **A**
   Dominus <u>cordī</u> <u>Christiānī</u> <u>pācem</u> dat.

   (The Lord gives the heart of the Christian peace.)

4.   **N**   **G**
   <u>Scriptūra</u> mihi viam <u>vēritātis</u> docet.

   (Scripture teaches me the way of truth.)

5. **A**   **D**   **N**
   <u>Vītam</u> aeternam dat <u>nōbīs</u> <u>Deus</u>.

   (God gives us eternal life.)

A. Rewrite the underlined word in the first blank and then draw a vertical line to separate the case inflection from the stem.

B. In the remaining three blanks, give the requested information about the underlined noun, using the abbreviations shown.

meaning (supply English prepositions where they are needed)

case (Nom, Gen, Dat, Acc)

function (S, PN, DO, IO, Gen Mod)

1. Rōma est magna <u>urbs</u>.

urb / s	city	Nom	PN

2. Nōmen <u>urbis</u> est Rōma.

urb / is	of the city	Gen	Gen Mod

3. Fīlius <u>agricolae</u> est Tullius.

agricol / ae	farmer's / of the farmer	Gen	Gen Mod

4. <u>Agricolae</u> pecūniam° dominus dat.

agricol / ae	to the farmer / the farmer	Dat	IO

[°money]

5. Agricola <u>fīliō</u> pecūniam dat.   **Accept *his son* for *the son*.**

fīli / ō	to the son / the son	Dat	IO

6. Agricola <u>quercuī</u> aquam° dat.

querc / uī	to the oak tree / the oak tree	Dat	IO

[°water]

7. Christus <u>peccātōrī</u> viam ostendit.

peccātōr / ī	to the sinner / the sinner	Dat	IO

8. Christus peccātōrī <u>viam</u> ostendit.

vi / am	the way	Acc	DO

9. Christus peccātōrī <u>spem</u> dat.

sp / em	hope	Acc	DO

© 1999 BJU Press. Reproduction prohibited.

Write Latin answers to these questions, which are based on the sentences in Activity F. In questions 1, 3, 5, and 6, omit the noun subject since it is clearly understood in the question. The verb inflection shows what the subject is, as you have seen in earlier chapters.

> Statement: Dominus mihi victōriam dat.   **(The Lord gives me victory.)**
> Question: Cui Dominus victōriam dat?   **(To whom does the Lord give victory?)**
> Answer: Mihi victōriam dat.   **(He gives me victory.)**

Do not omit other words in your sentence answers. In sentence 1, *Verbum* is in the nominative case. In Chapter 8 you will learn why it is nominative even though it looks like an accusative form.

1. Cui Verbum Deī vēritātem ostendit? _____

    *Mihi/Tibi/Nōbīs/Christiānō vēritātem ostendit. / Verbum Deī mihi. . . .*

    (To whom does the Word of God show truth?)

2. Quid mihi vēritātem ostendit? _____

    *Verbum Deī mihi vēritātem ostendit.*

    (What shows me truth?)

3. Cui Christus veniam praebet? _____

    *Peccātōrī veniam praebet. / Christus peccātōrī. . . .*

    (To whom does Christ offer pardon?)

4. Quis cordī peccātōris pācem dat? _____

    *Dominus/Christus/Deus cordī peccātōris pācem dat.*

    (Who gives peace to the heart of a sinner?)

5. Cui Scriptūra viam vēritātis docet? _____

    *Mihi/Tibi/Christiānō viam vēritātis docet. / Scriptūra mihi/tibi/Christiānō. . . .*

    (To whom does Scripture show the way of truth?)

6. Docetne Scriptūra mihi viam vēritātis? _____

    *Tibi viam vēritātis docet. / Scriptūra tibi. . . .*

    (Does Scripture teach me the way of truth?)

© 1999 BJU Press. Reproduction prohibited.

Activity I

Read each Latin statement and then write a brief answer in Latin to the question or questions that follow.

1. Rōma mundō linguam Latīnam dedit. Cui Rōma linguam Latīnam dedit? _____*mundō*_____
   (Rome gave the world the Latin language. / Rome gave the Latin language to the world. To whom did Rome give the Latin language?)

2. Fīliō pater stilum dat. Cui pater stilum dat? _____*fīliō*_____
   (The father gives the son a stylus. / The father gives a stylus to the son. To whom does the father give the stylus?

3. Stilum pater fīliō dat. Quis nunc° stilum habet? _____*fīlius*_____
   (The father gives the son a stylus. Who now has a stylus?)
   [°now]

4. Puer magistrō grātiam ostendit. Quis magistrō grātiam ostendit? _____*puer*_____

   Cui puer grātiam ostendit? _____*magistrō*_____
   (The boy shows gratitude to the teacher. / The boy shows the teacher gratitude. To whom does the boy show gratitude?)

5. Magister discipulō librum praebet. Quis discipulō librum praebet? _____*magister*_____

   Cui magister librum praebet? _____*discipulō*_____
   (The teacher offers the pupil a/the book. / The teacher offers a/the book to the pupil. Who offers the pupil a/the book? To whom does the teacher offer a/the book?)

Activity J

Give two translations for each sentence, showing the two ways that the dative case can be translated.

1. Magister discipulō historiam° Rōmae docet. _____*The teacher teaches the pupil the history of Rome. / The teacher teaches the history of Rome to the pupil.*_____
   [°history]

2. Senātor patriae spem dat. _____*The senator gives the country hope. / The senator gives hope to the country.*_____

3. Patria nominī senātōris honōrem° dat. _____*The country gives the name of the senator honor. / The country gives honor to the name of the senator.*_____
   [°honor]

4. Rēx victōrī honōrem dat. _____*The king gives the victor honor. / The king gives honor to the victor.*_____

5. Victor vulgō ōrātiōnem° dat. _____*The victor gives the masses/multitude/crowd a speech. / The victor gives a speech to the multitude.*_____
   [°speech, oration]

© 1999 BJU Press. Reproduction prohibited.

© 1999 BJU Press. Reproduction prohibited.

Activity K

Fill in the blanks, using the dative form that means the same as the phrase under the line. In Chapter 3 you saw that the Spanish word for "God" is *Dios,* and the French word is *Dieu.*

1. _____*Cui*_____ est verbum *Dios* similis?
   to what
   (To what is the word *Dios* similar?)

2. Verbum *Dios* est similis _____*verbō*_____ *Dieu.*
   to the word
   (The word *Dios* is similar to the word *Dieu.*)

3. _____*Cui*_____ est Christiānus bonus fidēlis?
   to whom
   (To whom is a good Christian faithful?)

4. Christiānus bonus est fidēlis _____*Dominō*_____.
   to the Lord
   (A good Christian is faithful to the Lord.)

5. _____*Cui*_____ est senātor° amīcus?
   to whom
   [°senator]   **(To whom is the senator friendly?)**

6. Senātor est amīcus _____*rēgī*_____.
   to the king
   (The senator is friendly to the king.)

Activity L

In each blank write the Latin word that translates the phrase under the line.

1. Pastor _____*Verbō*_____ Deī est fidēlis.
   to the Word
   (The pastor is faithful to the Word of God.)

2. Pastor _____*nōbīs*_____ vēritātem ostendit.
   us/to us
   (The pastor shows us truth.)

3. Pater meus est _____*amīcus*_____ pastōrī.
   friendly
   (My father is friendly to the pastor.)

4. Sum quoque amīcus _____*pastōrī*_____.
   to the pastor
   (I am also friendly to the pastor.)

For each of these English words, write the Latin word that helps you understand the derivative. For each Latin *noun* you give, write both the nominative and genitive forms. In the second blank write the meaning of the Latin word.

1. amicable _____ amīcus _____ friendly _____
2. cordial _____ cor, cordis _____ heart _____
3. duke _____ dux, ducis _____ general/leader _____
4. fidelity _____ fidēlis _____ faithful _____
5. gratitude _____ grātia, grātiae _____ grace/gratitude _____
6. lucid _____ lūx, lūcis _____ light _____
7. senatorial _____ senātor, senātōris _____ senator _____
8. similarity _____ similis _____ similar _____
9. verbose _____ verbum, verbī _____ word _____
10. verity _____ vēritās, vēritātis _____ truth _____

For each of these English words, write the Latin word, with its meaning, from which the English word comes. This review activity includes words from Chapters 1-4.

1. librarian _____ liber _____ book _____
2. urban _____ urbs _____ city _____
3. discipline _____ discit/discipula/discipulus _____ learns/pupil _____
4. Deity _____ Deus _____ God _____
5. vitality _____ vīta _____ life _____
6. filial _____ fīlius _____ son _____
7. glorious _____ glōria _____ glory _____
8. ostensible _____ ostendit _____ shows _____
9. mundane _____ mundus _____ world _____
10. population _____ populus _____ people _____

© 1999 BJU Press. Reproduction prohibited.

© 1999 BJU Press. Reproduction prohibited.

Activity O

This vocabulary review covers words from this chapter and from Chapters 1-4. The contexts should help you remember the meanings of the words. Some of the phrases contain adjectives or genitive-case nouns (after the nouns they modify), and some items contain dative-case nouns (before the direct object or the special adjective). Write each phrase or sentence in English.

1. cor senātōris _____ *the heart of the senator* _____

2. dux vulgī _____ *the leader of the multitude/masses/mob* _____

3. truncus quercūs _____ *the trunk of an oak tree* _____

4. vēritās Scriptūrae _____ *the truth of Scripture* _____

5. grātia Deī _____ *the grace of God* _____

6. Agnus Deī _____ *the Lamb of God* _____

7. rēgī fidēlis _____ *faithful to the king* _____

8. tibi similis _____ *similar to you* _____

9. mihi amīcus _____ *friendly to me* _____

10. Deus peccātōrī veniam dat. _____ *God gives pardon to a sinner.* _____

11. Victor patriae pācem dat. _____ *The victor gives peace to the country.* _____

12. Dux vulgō ōrātiōnem dat. _____ *The leader gives a speech to the multitude/masses/mob.* _____

13. Victor rēgī honōrem praebet. _____ *The victor offers honor to the king.* _____

14. Deus nōbīs grātiam praebet. _____ *God offers grace to us.* _____

Here is more vocabulary review of words in this and earlier chapters. From the list of verbs, write the correct one in each blank. *Secundus* is the subject of the first sentence. After that, each subject is the understood pronoun *he*.

dat	dīligit	erat	legit
dedit	discit	est	ostendit
dēfendit	docet	timet	pascit
dīcit	dūcit	habet	praebet

1. Secundus teaches. Secundus _____*docet*_____.

2. He learns. _____*Discit*_____.

3. He speaks. _____*Dīcit*_____.

4. He leads. _____*Dūcit*_____.

5. He defends. _____*Dēfendit*_____.

6. He offers. _____*Praebet*_____.

7. He shows. _____*Ostendit*_____.

8. He feeds. _____*Pascit*_____.

9. He gives. _____*Dat*_____.

10. He was. _____*Erat*_____.

11. He fears. _____*Timet*_____.

12. He gave. _____*Dedit*_____.

13. He is. _____*Est*_____.

14. He reads. _____*Legit*_____.

15. He has. _____*Habet*_____.

16. He loves. _____*Dīligit*_____.

© 1999 BJU Press. Reproduction prohibited.

CAPITULUM VII

© 1999 BJU Press. Reproduction prohibited.

Activity A

Without looking at the text, complete each statement by filling in the blanks. When you have completed the activity, check what you have written by looking at the text; write any needed corrections above your original answers.

1. The famous Roman authors Julius Caesar and _____ *Cicero* _____
   were also _____ *military* _____ and political leaders.

2. In the New Testament, Octavius Caesar is called by his title _____ *Augustus* _____.
   This title means _____ *majestic / inspiring awe* _____.

3. The poet who wrote the *Aeneid* was _____ *Virgil/Vergil* _____.

4. Three other well-known Roman poets were _____ *Horace* _____,
   _____ *Martial* _____, and _____ *Catullus* _____.

5. The *Aeneid* is a/an _____ *epic* _____ poem, which tells about _____
   the legendary history of Rome _____.

Activity B

Write each of these nouns in the four remaining cases. In the second blank for each word, give the English meaning. If you have forgotten the meaning of any word, an English derivative may remind you. If necessary, you may check the Vocābulārium.

1. via, _____ *viae, viae, viam, viā* _____   *road, way*

2. stilus, _____ *stilī, stilō, stilum, stilō* _____   *pen*

3. canis, _____ *canis, canī, canem, cane* _____   *dog*

4. senātus, _____ *senātūs, senātuī, senātum, senātū* _____   *senate*

5. spēs, _____ *speī, speī, spem, spē* _____   *hope*

Activity C

Translate each sentence and then make your English translation more interesting by adding one or more prepositional phrases. **Answers will vary.**

1. Puer ambulat. _____ *The/A boy is walking / walks in the woods / near the lake / on the sand.* _____

2. Canis currit. _____ *The dog runs behind him.* _____

3. Fīlius magistrī natat. _____ *The teacher's son swims in the lake.* _____

4. Arbor stat. _____ *The tree stands on the beach.* _____

5. Truncus arboris iacet. _____ *The trunk of the tree lies on the ground.* _____

6. Magister sedet. _____ *The teacher sits on the trunk of the tree.* _____

Activity D

Write these phrases in English.

1. via ā silvā _____ *a/the road/way from / away from the forest* _____

2. via dē silvā _____ *road down from the forest* _____

3. via ē silvā _____ *road out from the forest* _____

4. via in silvam _____ *road into the forest* _____

5. via per silvam _____ *road through the forest* _____

6. via trāns insulam _____ *road across the island* _____

7. lacus ad silvam _____ *lake near/at the forest* _____

8. lupus in silvā _____ *wolf in the forest* _____

9. puer sine cane _____ *boy without a dog* _____

10. puer cum cane _____ *boy with a dog* _____

11. diēs ante moram _____ *time/day before the delay* _____

12. diēs post moram _____ *time/day after the delay* _____

© 1999 BJU Press. Reproduction prohibited.

Activity E

Write each prepositional phrase in Latin. Be careful to use the correct form of *ē* or *ex* and *ā* or *ab*. The word *woods* in English is a plural form, but the Latin word with that meaning is singular in form.

1. in the woods _____ *in silvā* _____

2. through the woods _____ *per silvam* _____

3. out from the woods _____ *ē silvā* _____

4. with the boy _____ *cum puerō* _____

5. across the island _____ *trāns insulam* _____

6. into the water _____ *in aquam* _____

7. near the water _____ *ad aquam* _____

8. toward the land _____ *ad terram* _____

9. away from the lake _____ *ā lacū* _____

10. on the trunk of a tree _____ *in truncō arboris* _____

Activity F

These Latin prepositional phrases are taken from the writings of Julius Caesar. Choose the meaning of each phrase from the English list below and write it in the blank. Some of the nouns are new to you. Make reasonable guesses. These English derivatives provide clues for the meanings of some words: *vigilance* (watchfulness), *itinerary* (route for a journey), *hostile*, and *mortuary*. (You will not be responsible for these new Latin words until they appear in later chapters.)

upon the mountain	from the lake
through our Province	on the journey
into the Rhone river	away from the enemy
from the third watch	in the sight of our army
near Geneva	after the death of the senator

1. in itinere _____ *on the journey* _____

2. per Provinciam nostram _____ *through our Province* _____

3. ad Genāvam _____ *near Geneva* _____

4. ā lacū _____ *from the lake* _____

5. in flūmen Rhodanum _____ *into the Rhone river* _____

6. in conspectū exercitūs nostrī _____ *in the sight of our army* _____

7. dē tertiā vigiliā _____ *from the third watch* _____

8. in montem _____ *upon the mountain* _____

9. post mortem senātōris _____ *after the death of the senator* _____

10. ab hoste _____ *away from the enemy* _____

© 1999 BJU Press. Reproduction prohibited.

Translate these sentences into Latin. Check the list of prepositions when necessary in order to be sure that you are using the correct case for the object of each preposition. Also be careful to use macrons where they are needed.

1. Quintus swims in the lake. _____

   _____ *Quintus in lacū natat.* _____

2. He swims across the lake. _____

   _____ *Trāns lacum natat.* _____

3. The pupil sits on the trunk of a tree. _____

   _____ *Discipulus/Discipula in truncō arboris sedet.* _____

4. The trunk of the tree is lying on the sand. _____

   _____ *Truncus arboris in hārēnā iacet.* _____

5. The dog runs after the mouse. _____

   _____ *Canis post mūrem currit.* _____

6. The elephant walks in the forest. _____

   _____ *Elephantus in silvā ambulat.* _____

© 1999 BJU Press. Reproduction prohibited.

For each word give the meaning, the case, and the function(s) of that case. Use the abbreviations listed. Keep this information in mind as you work:

a. Objects of prepositions may be in either the accusative or the ablative case.

b. In the first and fifth declensions, the genitive and dative inflections are the same.

c. In the second declension the dative and ablative inflections are the same.

N (nominative)	S (subject)
G (genitive)	Mod (possessive or the English *of* phrase)
D (dative)	IO (indirect object or used with special adjective)
Acc (accusative)	DO (direct object)
Abl (ablative)	OP (object of a preposition)

1. arbore	*tree*	*Abl*	*OP*
2. agnō	*lamb*	*D, Abl*	*IO / with sp. adj. / OP*
3. honōrem	*honor*	*Acc*	*DO, OP*
4. senātōris	*senator*	*G*	*Mod*
5. corde	*heart*	*Abl*	*OP*
6. vulgō	*multitude*	*D, Abl*	*IO / with sp. adj. / OP*
7. speī	*hope*	*G, D*	*Mod / IO / with sp. adj.*
8. veniā	*pardon*	*Abl*	*OP*
9. venia	*pardon*	*N*	*S*
10. urbem	*city*	*Acc*	*DO, OP*

Activity I

Label each underlined word or phrase according to its case in the sentence. Then translate each sentence. The meanings of the new words are obvious from English derivatives.

N (nominative)	Acc (accusative)
G (genitive)	Abl (ablative)
D (dative)	

1. <u>Graecia°</u> est ad <u>Ītaliam°</u>.   *Greece is near Italy.*
   [°Greece; °Italy]
   N ... *Acc*

2. Graecia est in <u>Eurōpā°</u>.   *Greece is in Europe.*
   [°Europe]
   Abl

3. Lingua <u>Graeciae</u> est similis <u>linguae Latīnae</u>.
   G ... *D*

   The language of Greece / Greek language is similar to the Latin language.

© 1999 BJU Press. Reproduction prohibited.

4. Magistra mea $\overset{D}{\underline{\text{mihi}}}$ $\overset{Acc}{\underline{\text{linguam Anglicam}}}$ docet. _____

_____ *My teacher teaches me the English language.*

5. $\overset{N}{\underline{\text{Historia}}}$ $\overset{D}{\underline{\text{nōbīs}}}$ dē $\overset{Abl}{\underline{\text{Rōmā}}}$ docet. _____

History teaches us about Rome.

6. Cicero $\overset{D}{\underline{\text{senātuī}}}$ $\overset{G}{\underline{\text{Rōmae}}}$ $\overset{Acc}{\underline{\text{ōrātiōnem}}}$ dedit. _____

Cicero gave a speech (an oration) to the senate of Rome.

_____

Activity J

Read each sentence and write a brief Latin answer to the question that follows it. Use the case inflection that you would use if you answered with a complete sentence.

1. Sciūrus° dē arbore currit.

   Ubi° sciūrus currit? _____ *dē arbore* _____

   [°squirrel; °where] **The squirrel runs down from the tree. Where does the squirrel run?**

2. Cum cane Marcus currit.

   Quis cum cane currit? _____ *Marcus* _____
   Marcus runs with the dog. Who runs with the dog?

3. Amīcus Marcī ē silvā ambulat.

   Cuius amīcus ē silvā ambulat? _____ *Marcī / amīcus Marcī* _____
   Marcus's friend walks out of the forest. Whose friend walks out of the forest?

4. Iulius in lacū natat.

   Ubi Iulius natat? _____ *in lacū* _____
   Julius swims in the lake. Where does Julius swim?

5. Canis in aquam insilit°.

   Ubi canis insilit? _____ *in aquam* _____
   [°jumps] **The dog jumps into the water. Where does the dog jump?**

6. Iulius cum cane trāns lacum ad silvam natat.

   Ad quid Iulius natat? _____ *ad silvam* _____
   Julius swims with the dog across the lake to the forest. To what does Julius swim?

7. Tum° per silvam puer ambulat.

   Ubi puer ambulat? _____ *per silvam* _____
   [°then] **Then the boy walks through the forest. Where does the boy walk?**

8. Iulius est fīlius senātōris.

   Quis est pater Iulī? _____ *senātor* _____
   Julius is the son of a/the senator. Who is Julius's father?

9. Post conventum pater cum fīliō ad lacum ambulat.

   Quis post conventum cum Iuliō ambulat? _____ *pater / pater Iuliī/Iulī* _____
   After the meeting the father walks with Julius to the lake. Who walks with Julius after the meeting?

© 1999 BJU Press. Reproduction prohibited.

A. Think about the meanings of these sentences. In sentences 1, 3, and 4, decide what is being compared. In sentence 3, decide what brings about *glōria,* or what *glōria* is the result of. In sentence 4, decide what the metaphor says about people.

B. Translate each sentence. All the cases that you have learned are included in the sentences. In sentence 3 the normal word order is used: *virtūtis* modifies *umbra.* Remember to supply *est* when it is missing.

1. Vīta nostra° similis bullae° in aquā. (Culman, 17th century) _____ *Our life is similar to a* _____ *bubble in water.* **(In other words, our life is very brief and easily extinguished.)**

    [°our; °bubble]

2. Nēmo° sine vitiō° est. (Seneca, first century) _____ *Nobody is without a fault.* _____

    [°nobody; °fault]

3. Glōria umbra° virtūtis°. (Seneca) _____ *Glory is the shadow of virtue.* _____ **(In other words, glory results from a virtuous life.)**

    [°shadow; °virtue]

4. Lupus nōn mordet° lupum. (Anonymous medieval author) _____ *A wolf does not bite a wolf.* **(In other words, people do not hurt other people who are like themselves.)**

    [°does bite]

5. Remedium° īrae° est mora°. (Seneca) _____ *The remedy of anger is delay.* **(A similar English saying is "Count to ten before you speak.")**

    [°remedy; °anger; °delay]

From the sentences in Activity K, list the words requested.

1. four first-declension nouns in the nominative case _____ *vīta, glōria, umbra, mora*

2. one second-declension noun in the nominative case _____ *lupus/remedium*

3. two nouns in the genitive case _____ *virtūtis, īrae*

4. one noun in the dative case _____ *bullae*

5. one noun in the accusative case _____ *lupum*

6. two nouns in the ablative case _____ *aquā, vitiō*

7. one predicate noun _____ *umbra/mora*

8. one direct object _____ *lupum*

9. one adverb _____ *nōn*

Written exercises 49

© 1999 BJU Press. Reproduction prohibited.

This activity has two sections. In each section, write the letter for the meaning of each word or phrase. Each definition contains the meaning or a suggestion of the meaning of the Latin word from which the derivative comes. Loan words and phrases are underlined.

Part 1

_____D_____ 1. territory   A. characteristic of a forest

_____F_____ 2. aqua pura   B. standing

_____C_____ 3. ambulatory   C. able to walk

_____A_____ 4. sylvan   D. land

_____G_____ 5. terra firma   E. across the Atlantic

_____B_____ 6. stationary   F. pure water

_____E_____ 7. transatlantic   G. solid ground

Part 2

_____C_____ 1. sedentary   A. an indoor swimming pool

_____E_____ 2. current   B. growing in water

_____B_____ 3. aquatic   C. requiring much sitting (such as a job or a hobby)

_____G_____ 4. insulate   D. a room one enters before entering other rooms

_____D_____ 5. anteroom   E. onward movement, as of water

_____A_____ 6. natatorium   F. a sandy area used for sports contests

_____F_____ 7. arena   G. to place in a detached or separated situation

© 1999 BJU Press. Reproduction prohibited.

Write in the first blank the Latin word from which part or all of each English word originated; in the second blank, give the meaning of the Latin word.

1. territory _____*terra*_____ _____*earth/soil/land*_____

2. ambulatory _____*ambulat*_____ _____*walks*_____

3. sylvan _____*silva*_____ _____*forest/woods*_____

4. stationary _____*stat*_____ _____*stands*_____

5. transfer _____*trāns*_____ _____*across*_____

6. concurrent _____*currit*_____ _____*runs*_____

7. aquarium _____*aqua*_____ _____*water*_____

8. insulation _____*insula*_____ _____*island*_____

9. antecedent _____*ante*_____ _____*before*_____

Activity O

This vocabulary review covers words from this chapter and from review chapters. The contexts should help you remember the meanings of the words. Translate each sentence into English. In sentence 5, *Flora* is the name of a girl.

1. Puer in truncō arboris sedet. _____

   The boy sits on the trunk of a tree.

2. Quintus in lacū natat. _____

   Quintus swims in the lake.

3. Marcus in umbrā arboris stat. _____

   Marcus stands in the shade/shadow of a tree.

4. Puer cum magistrō ambulat. _____

   The boy walks with the teacher.

5. Flōra in insulā vīvit°. _____

   Flora lives on an island.

   [°lives]

6. Timotheus ad lacum currit. _____

   Timothy runs to the lake.

7. Canis porcum mordet. _____

   The dog bites the pig.

8. Stilus ad librum iacet. _____

   The pen lies near the book.

© 1999 BJU Press. Reproduction prohibited.

9. Nēmō sine vitiō est. _____

_____**No one is without a fault.**_____

10. Remedium īrae est mora. _____

_____**The remedy of anger is delay.**_____

11. Vīta nostra [est] similis bullae in aquā. _____

_____**Our life is similar to a bubble in water.**_____

© 1999 BJU Press. Reproduction prohibited.

CAPITULUM VIII

© 1999 BJU Press. Reproduction prohibited.

Activity A

Give brief answers.

1. Was Rome a kingdom before or after the years that Christ lived on the earth?

    before

2. Was Rome a republic before or after the time of Christ?

    before

3. Who was ruling Rome when Christ was born and what was the ruler's title? (If you have forgotten, see the beginning of Chapter 4.)

    Augustus Caesar / Caesar Augustus was emperor.

4. Who established the empire that became the Byzantine Empire?

    Emperor Constantine

5. What important events occurred in A.D. 476 and A.D. 1453?

    The Western Roman Empire fell in A.D. 476.

    The Byzantine Empire fell in A.D. 1453.

6. Did most of the development of the Romance languages take place in the Eastern or the Western Roman Empire?

    in the Western Roman Empire

Translate these sentences. Remember that the agreement of an adjective with the word it modifies does not require identical spelling of the inflections. Since sentence 3 has three new words, you may need to look at the meanings of those words before you translate the sentence.

1. Parvus mūs ab cane currit. _____

    A/The small mouse runs from the dog.

2. Parvus elephantus magnum mūrem nōn videt. _____

    A/The small elephant does not see a/the large mouse.

3. Magistra bona investīgātiōnem° dūram° interdum° dat. _____

    A/The good teacher sometimes gives a hard examination.

    [°examination; °hard; °sometimes]

4. Senātor fidēlis viam honōris° ostendit. _____

    A/The faithful senator shows the way of honor.

    [°honor]

5. Victor virtūtem magnam habet. _____

    A/The victor has great courage/virtue.

Translate each sentence into Latin.

1. The Word of God is true. _____

    Verbum Deī est vērum.

2. Sin is in the world. _____

    Peccātum in mundō est.

3. The world does not love Christ. _____

    Mundus Christum nōn dīligit.

4. Christ loves the world. _____

    Christus mundum dīligit.

5. A Christian loves the name of the Savior. _____

    Christiānus nōmen Salvātōris dīligit.

© 1999 BJU Press. Reproduction prohibited.

Write these phrases in Latin, being careful to use the correct case inflections.

1. (subject) word of truth _____ *verbum vēritātis* _____
2. (indirect object) the leader of the country _____ *ducī patriae* _____
3. (subject) new book _____ *liber novus* _____
4. (direct object) a new beginning _____ *initium novum* _____
5. in the history of Rome _____ *in histōri Rōmae* _____
6. near the door _____ *ad ostium* _____
7. (subject) the remedy of a fault _____ *remedium vitī/vitiī* _____
8. (direct object) kind of bread _____ *genus panis* _____
9. (direct object) the time of day _____ *tempus diēī* _____
10. (indirect object) to/for the vast empire _____ *vastō imperiō* _____

Activity E

Supply an appropriate Latin adjective in each of these sentences. If necessary, look through the Essential Information sections of the first six chapters for adjectives you can use. Make the adjectives agree in case with the nouns they modify. Remember, the inflection of an adjective is not always spelled like the inflection of the modified noun. Answers will vary.

1. Iulius Caesar erat _____ *magnus/bonus/vērus* _____ dux Romānus.
   (Julius Caesar was a great/good/true Roman leader.)

2. Caesar erat quoque nōmen Augustī. Augustus erat dux _____ *Rōmānus/magnus/bonus/vērus* _____.
   (Caesar was also the name of Augustus. Augustus was a Roman/great/good/true leader.)

3. Lingua Iulī Caesaris erat lingua _____ *Latīna* _____.
   (The language of Julius Caesar / Julius Caesar's language was the Latin language.)

4. Tempus Iuliī Caesaris erat ante tempus Christī. Imperium Iuliī Caesaris erat
   _____ *magnum/vastum* _____. (The time of Julius Caesar was before the time of Christ. The power [to rule] of Julius Caesar was great/vast.)

5. Rōma _____ *bonum/magnum* _____ iūs habēbat.
   (Rome had good/great law.)

6. Opus Christī erat _____ *bonum/magnum* _____.
   (The work of Christ was good/great.)

© 1999 BJU Press. Reproduction prohibited.

Answer each question in a Latin sentence. When the subject is clear from what has been said previously and is implied in the verb inflection, it is customary to omit the noun subject. For question 4, use any Latin name in the answer.

1. Estne Antōnius amīcus tuus bonus? ___*Est / Nōn est amīcus bonus meus.*___

   _____

   (Is Antony/Anthony your good friend?)

2. Estne Antōnius fīlius magnī senātōris? ___*Est / Nōn est fīlius magnī senātōris.*___

   _____

   (Is Antony/Anthony the great senator's son?)

3. Vīvitne° in urbe? ___*Ita vērē in urbe vīvit. / Nōn in urbe vīvit.*___

   _____

   [°live] **(Does he live in the city?)**

4. Quis amīcō tuō linguam Anglicam docet? ___*Magistra Olivia amīcō meō linguam*___

   ___*Anglicam docet.*___

   (Who teaches your friend the English language?)

© 1999 BJU Press. Reproduction prohibited.

This activity uses derivatives to review vocabulary words presented in this chapter and previous chapters. In the first blank, write the Latin word from which the underlined word came. If the Latin word is a noun, write its nominative and genitive forms. In the second blank, write the meaning of the Latin word.

At first you may not see a relationship between the meaning of some Latin source words and the English derivatives. Let the sentence context be your clue and you will begin to better understand the meaning of the English word.

1. Before construction work begins, <u>initial</u> plans are studied and final plans are made.

   initium, -ī/iī   *beginning*

2. In <u>urban</u> areas construction work is nearly always in progress.

   urbs, urbis   *city*

3. As city <u>population</u> grows, the need for constructing new buildings increases.

   populus, -ī/iī   *people*

4. The <u>operation</u> of construction equipment replaces much manual labor.

   opus, operis   *work*

5. Even with the help of machines, construction companies need workers for <u>manual</u> labor.

   manus, -ūs   *hand*

6. <u>Temporary</u> buildings are often necessary for tool storage at construction sites.

   tempus, -poris   *time*

7. There is <u>real</u> danger if unqualified workers operate construction equipment.

   rēs, reī   *thing*

8. Electric wires must be carefully <u>insulated</u>.

   insula, -ae   *island*

© 1999 BJU Press. Reproduction prohibited.

Activity H

To review the new vocabulary in this chapter, write the Latin noun, its genitive form, and its gender for each English noun. Do not look at any vocabulary listing until you have completed the activity. Make any corrections in pencil if you wrote in ink and vice versa. Then *learn* the vocabulary information about any words which you answered incorrectly.

1. fault _____ *vitium, -iī/ī, n.* _____

2. right, law _____ *iūs, iūris / jūs, jūris, n.* _____

3. empire _____ *imperium, -iī/ī, n.* _____

4. sin _____ *peccatum, -ī, n.* _____

5. time _____ *tempus, -oris, n.* _____

6. work _____ *opus, operis, n.* _____

7. kind, class _____ *genus, -eris, n.* _____

8. name _____ *nōmen, -minis, n.* _____

9. beginning _____ *initium, -iī/ī, n.* _____

10. remedy _____ *remedium, -iī/ī, n.* _____

© 1999 BJU Press. Reproduction prohibited.

CAPITULUM IX

Give the gender of each class of nouns or each individual noun listed. You may use abbreviations *(m., f., n.)*.

___f.___ 1. most first-declension nouns

___m.___ 2. the nouns *agricola* and *prophēta*

___m.___ 3. most second-declension *-us* and *-er* nouns

___n.___ 4. second-declension *-um* nouns

___m.___ 5. most fourth-declension nouns

___f.___ 6. the noun *quercus*

___f.___ 7. most fifth-declension nouns

Activity B

Translate each noun phrase and in the second blank write the case of the words in the phrase. All the phrases are singular. If you have forgotten the meaning of any of these words, you may look them up in the Vocābulārium. Be sure to take time right now to learn the meaning of the words you look up so that you will not need to look them up again.

The adjective in each phrase agrees in gender as well as case with the noun it modifies. In the third blank, write the gender of that noun. You may abbreviate case *(nom., gen., dat., acc., abl.)* and gender names *(m., f., n.)*.

1. parva urbs ___small city___ ___nom.___ ___f.___

2. amīcum fidēlem ___faithful friend___ ___acc.___ ___m.___

3. patriā tuā ___your country___ ___abl.___ ___f.___

4. librī meī ___of my book / my book's___ ___gen.___ ___m.___

5. magnā urbe ___large city___ ___abl.___ ___f.___

6. magnae quercuī ___large oak tree___ ___dat.___ ___f.___

© 1999 BJU Press. Reproduction prohibited.

Activity C

Write the correct form of *bonus, -a, -um* after each noun. Make the adjective agree with the noun in gender and case. In number 5, two answers are required because *diēs* is sometimes masculine and sometimes feminine. In number 10, two answers are required because *vītis* has the same ending for two different cases.

1. aqua _____ *bona* _____

2. amīcō _____ *bonō* _____

3. pane _____ *bonō* _____

4. senātūs _____ *bonī* _____

5. diem _____ *bonam, bonum* _____

6. cordis _____ *bonī* _____

7. nōmen _____ *bonum* _____

8. stilus _____ *bonus* _____

9. librum _____ *bonum* _____

10. vītis _____ *bona, bonae* _____

© 1999 BJU Press. Reproduction prohibited.

Write each noun phrase in the genitive, dative, accusative, and ablative cases. Check the Vocābulārium for the gender of a noun if you have any doubt. Be careful to make the adjective agree with the noun whether the endings look alike or not. Remember that the noun *liber,* like *magister,* drops the *e* before the final *r.*

1. magna patria

magnae patriae

magnae patriae

magnam patriam

magnā patriā

2. agricola amicus

agricolae amīcī

agricolae amīcō

agricolam amīcum

agricolā amīcō

3. longus liber

longī librī

longō librō

longum librum

longō librō

4. dux tuus

ducis tuī

ducī tuō

ducem tuum

duce tuō

5. longum tempus

longī temporis

longō temporī

longum tempus

longō tempore

6. senātus Rōmānus

senatus Rōmānī

senātuī Rōmānō

senātum Rōmānum

senātū Rōmānō

7. longa diēs

longae diēī

longae diēī

longam diem

longā diē

© 1999 BJU Press. Reproduction prohibited.

Write these phrases in Latin, being careful to spell the stem of each adjective correctly.

1. free country (subject) _____ *patria lībera* _____

2. free poet (subject) _____ *poēta līber* _____

3. free country (direct object) _____ *patriam līberam* _____

4. free poet (direct object) _____ *poētam līberum* _____

5. our country (object of a preposition) _____ *patriā nostrā* _____

6. our horse (indirect object) _____ *equō nostrō* _____

7. large dog (possessive) _____ *magnī canis* _____

8. large tree (direct object) _____ *magnam arborem* _____

Activity F

Translate each sentence. Be prepared to give orally the case and gender of each noun and to name each adjective and its case and gender.

1. Verbum Deī est vēritās aeterna. _____ *The Word of God is eternal truth.* _____

   (nom., neut; gen., masc.; nom., fem.; —*aeterna*, nom., fem.)

2. Nōmen Deī est aeternum. _____ *The name of God is eternal.* _____

   (nom., neut.; gen., masc.; —*aeternum*, nom., neut.)

3. Hic mundus nōn est aeternus. (See Revelation 21:1.) _____ *This world is not eternal.* _____

   (nom., masc.; —*aeternus*, nom., masc.)

4. Christus est magnus Rēx. _____ *Christ is the great King.* _____

   (nom., masc.; nom., masc.; —*magnus*, nom., masc.)

5. Salvator Christiānō spem magnam dat. _____ *The Savior gives great*

   _____ *hope to a/the Christian. / The Savior gives a/the Christian great hope.* _____

   (nom., masc.; dat., masc.; acc., fem.; —*magnam*, acc., fem.)

© 1999 BJU Press. Reproduction prohibited.

Answer each question in Latin. Use complete sentences even if the subjects are clearly understood. The purpose of this activity is to give you practice in adjective-noun agreement. In some answers you may want to include the Latin equivalent for *yes, certainly.*

1. Eratne agricola bonus in rē publicā antīquā Rōmānā? _____

    Ita vērē, agricola bonus erat in rēpublicā antīquā Rōmānā.
    _____

    (Was there a / Was the good farmer in the ancient Roman republic?)

2. Eratne Imperium Rōmānum vastum? _____

    Ita vērē, Imperium Rōmānum erat vastum.
    _____

    (Was the Roman Empire vast?)

3. Eratne tempus Imperī Rōmānī longum aut breve°? _____

    Tempus Imperī Rōmānī erat longum.
    _____

    [°short] **(Was the time of the Roman Empire long or short?)**

4. Eratne Hispānia° antīqua in Imperiō Rōmānō? _____

    Ita vērē, Hispānia antīqua erat in Imperiō Rōmānō.
    _____

    [°Spain] **(Was ancient Spain in the Roman Empire?)**

5. Quis erat imperātor° prīmus° Imperī Rōmānī? _____

    Augustus Caesar / Caesar Augustus erat imperātor prīmus Imperī/Imperiī Rōmānī.
    _____

    [°emperor; °first] **(Who was the first emperor of the Roman Empire?)**

Choose the word or phrase that best completes each sentence and write it in the blank. The meanings and case endings of the words listed are your clue to where the words/phrases fit correctly. Do not use a word or phrase more than once.

Augustī Caesaris	America
Iulius Caesar	rēgem
Hispānia	Rēs publica
Ītaliā	Imperiō Rōmānō

1. Rōma est in _____ *Ītaliā* _____ .
    (Rome is in Italy.)

2. _____ *America* _____ nōn erat in Imperiō Rōmānō.
    (America was not in the Roman Empire.)

3. _____ *Hispānia* _____ erat in Imperiō Rōmānō.
    (Spain was in the Roman Empire.)

© 1999 BJU Press. Reproduction prohibited.

4. _____Iulius Caesar_____ erat dux magnus Rōmānus.

   (Julius Caesar was a great Roman leader.)

5. Vīta Christī in mundō erat in tempore _____Augustī Caesaris_____.

   (The life of Christ in the world was in the time of Augustus Caesar.)

6. Prīmō Rōma _____rēgem_____ habēbat.

   (At first Rome had a king.)

7. _____Rēs publica_____ Rōmae erat ante tempus Christī.

   (The republic of Rome was before the time of Christ.)

8. Christiānus in _____Imperiō Rōmānō_____ vītam dūram habēbat.

   (A Christian had a hard life in the Roman Empire.)

Activity I

Write the letter for the meaning that matches the Latin phrase. (The long vowels are *not* marked with macrons because these are now English expressions. Macrons, you may recall, were not used by the Romans. In Latin books, they are an aid as you learn to pronounce Latin.)

____L____ 1. ex tempore   A. with a grain of salt

____A____ 2. cum grano salis   B. truth conquers

____C____ 3. magnum opus   C. a great work

____K____ 4. magnum bonum   D. pure water

____H____ 5. mea culpa   E. a rare bird

____F____ 6. pater patriae   F. father of the country

____J____ 7. Pater noster   G. While there is life, there is hope.

____I____ 8. per diem   H. my fault

____E____ 9. rara avis   I. per day (daily)

____B____ 10. veritas vincit   J. Our Father (the Lord's Prayer)

____G____ 11. Dum vita est spes est.   K. great good

____D____ 12. aqua pura   L. from the time (without previous planning)

© 1999 BJU Press. Reproduction prohibited.

© 1999 BJU Press. Reproduction prohibited.

Activity J

This activity will help you understand some English derivatives of Latin words you have worked with. In the first blank, write the Latin word that suggests the meaning of the underlined word. If the Latin word is a noun, give both the nominative and the genitive forms. In the second blank, write the meaning of the word.

1. Bill expressed a <u>cordial</u> interest in the new student.

   _____cor, cordis_____   _____heart_____

2. As a Christian, he was interested in eternal matters, not just <u>temporal</u> matters.

   _____tempus, -oris_____   _____time_____

3. A district court does not have <u>jurisdiction</u> over matters outside the boundaries

   of its district. _____iūs, iūris / dīcit_____   _____right, law / says, speaks_____

4. The family showed Christian <u>fortitude</u> when their home was destroyed by a tornado.

   _____forte_____   _____strong_____

5. The audience appreciated the <u>brevity</u> of the man's speech.

   _____breve_____   _____short_____

Activity K

In the first blank, give the Latin origin of the English words; in numbers 2-5 include the gender endings of first- and second-declension adjectives.

In the second blank, give the meaning of the Latin word. If necessary, you may look at the vocabulary lists in Essential Information.

1. brevity, brief, abbreviate _____brevis_____   _____short_____

2. neutrality, neutralize _____neuter, -tra, -trum_____   _____neither one nor the other / neither male nor female_____

3. magnitude, magnify, magnificent _____magnus, -a, -um_____   _____large, great_____

4. primary, prime, primer _____prīmus, -a, -um_____   _____first_____

5. liberty, liberate, liberal _____līber, -bera, -berum_____   _____free_____

Written exercises   **65**

Match these review vocabulary words with their meanings.

_____C_____ 1. arbor, -oris, *f.*   A. name

_____I_____ 2. īra, īrae, *f.*   B. forgiveness

_____A_____ 3. nōmen, -inis, *n.*   C. tree

_____H_____ 4. opus, -eris, *n.*   D. thing

_____F_____ 5. peccātum, -ī, *n.*   E. hope

_____D_____ 6. rēs, reī, *f.*   F. sin

_____E_____ 7. spēs, speī, *f.*   G. shadow

_____G_____ 8. umbra, -ae, *f.*   H. work

_____B_____ 9. venia, -ae, *f.*   I. anger

© 1999 BJU Press. Reproduction prohibited.

CAPITULUM X

© 1999 BJU Press. Reproduction prohibited.

Activity A

Complete each sentence by filling in the blank. **Answers may vary slightly.**

1. The parent language of Spanish is the _____ Latin _____ language.

2. The parent language of Latin is the _____ Indo-European _____ language.

3. Two cognate languages of Spanish are _____ French/Italian/Portuguese/Romanian/Romansch _____.

4. Two cognate languages of Latin are _____ Greek/German/any other language on chart, p. 127 _____.

5. The Latin cognate of the German word *Maus* is _____ mūs _____.

6. In Latin and Greek, the cognate of the English word *me* is _____ me _____.

Activity B

Write each noun phrase in the oblique cases (all the cases after the nominative). You will be making a third-declension adjective agree with a noun in each of the five declensions (two third-declension nouns). Noun and adjective inflections often differ.

1. lingua facilis

   linguae facilis

   linguae facilī

   linguam facilem

   linguā facilī

2. verbum facile

   verbī facilis

   verbō facilī

   verbum facile

   verbō facilī

3. opus facile

   operis facilis

   operī facilī

   opus facile

   opere facilī

4. dux fortis

   ducis fortis

   ducī fortī

   ducem fortem

   duce fortī

5. quercus fortis

   quercūs fortis

   quercuī fortī

   quercum fortem

   quercū fortī

6. diēs facilis

   diēī facilis

   diēī facilī

   diem facilem

   diē facilī

Activity C

Write each noun phrase in the nominative case. Make the adjective agree with the noun in gender and case. *Spiritus* is masculine; *tempus* is neuter; *equus* is masculine.

1. bitter spirit _____ *spiritus acer* _____

2. short time _____ *tempus breve* _____

3. quick work _____ *opus celere* _____

4. swift horse _____ *equus celer* _____

5. quick pupil _____ *discipulus celer / discipula celeris* _____

Activity D

Write each noun phrase in Latin.

1. old farmer (subject) _____ *agricola vetus* _____

2. old name (subject) _____ *nōmen vetus* _____

3. of an old friend _____ *amīcī veteris* _____

4. old senator (indirect object) _____ *senātōrī veterī* _____

5. an old remedy (direct object) _____ *remedium vetus* _____

6. an old city (direct object) _____ *urbem veterem* _____

7. in an old lake _____ *in lacū veterī* _____

© 1999 BJU Press. Reproduction prohibited.

Answer the following questions.

1. What is the stem for each of these adjectives?

   a. līber, lībera, līberum _____ *līber-*

   b. acer, acris, acre _____ *acr-*

   c. audāx, audācis _____ *audāc-*

   d. tristis, triste _____ *trist-*

   e. noster, nostra, nostrum _____ *nostr-*

   f. vetus, *gen.* veteris _____ *veter-*

2. What is the alternate spelling of these words?

   a. iustus _____ *justus*

   b. iniustus _____ *injustus*

© 1999 BJU Press. Reproduction prohibited.

Write the meaning of each sentence. Besides the words that are defined below the answer blanks, you will find three other new words. They are so similar to their English meanings that they should pose no problem for you.

1. Patria est fidēlis rēgī. _____

   _____
   The country is faithful to the king.

2. Ille rēx iustus populum patriae dīligit. _____

   _____
   That just king loves the people of the country.

3. In brevī ōrātiōne rēx magnus dē honōre dīcit. _____

   _____
   In a brief oration/speech the great king speaks about honor.

4. Dux fortis exercitum° ad victōriam dūcit. _____

   _____
   The brave general leads the army to victory.

   [°army]

5. Victōria nōn est celer et nōn est facilis. _____

   _____
   The victory / Victory is not swift/quick, and it is not easy.

6. Post breve tempus dux vetus patriam iterum° dēfendit. _____

   _____
   After a brief time the old/experienced general again defends the country.

   [°again]

7. Patria vasta in pāce nunc° vīvit°. _____

   _____
   The vast country now lives in peace.

   [°now; °live]

© 1999 BJU Press. Reproduction prohibited.

Give the English meaning of each sentence.

1. Omnis senātor vetus in senātū dīcit. _____

   Every old senator speaks in the senate.

2. In brevī tristī ōrātiōne, Octāvius dē bellō° narrat°. _____

   In a short sad oration, Octavius tells about the war.

   [°war, °tell]

3. Senātor iuvenis quoque° in senātū dīcit. Est fīlius Octāvī. _____

   A young senator also speaks in the senate. He is the son of Octavius.

   [°also]

4. Nōmen senātōris iuvenis est Quintus. Quintus est similis Octāviō. _____

   The name of the young senator is Quintus. Quintus is similar to Octavius.

5. Rōma est patria Octāvī et Quintī. Rōma patriam potentem inimīcam° nōn vincit.

   Rome is the country of Octavius and Quintus.

   Rome does not conquer the powerful enemy country.

   [°enemy (adj.)]

6. Quintus est iuvenis et audāx; in ōrātiōne gravī dē bellō dīcit. _____

   Quintus is young and bold; in a serious oration he speaks about the war.

© 1999 BJU Press. Reproduction prohibited.

Activity H

Answer each question with a Latin sentence. Undefined new words are so similar to their English meanings that you can easily understand them. **Answers for questions 1, 2, and 7 will vary. Carefully check the agreement of adjectives with the nouns they modify. In questions 5 and 6, answers can begin with *ita vērē*.**

1. Quāle imperium erat Rōma? _____

   Rōma erat vastum/magnum/forte imperium.

   (What kind of empire was Rome?)

2. Quālis urbs est Rōma nunc°? _____

   Rōma est magna/lībera urbs nunc.

   [°now] **(What kind of city is Rome now?)**

3. Estne Rōma in Eurōpā aut in Āsiā? _____

   Rōma est in Eurōpā.

   (Is Rome in Europe or in Asia?)

4. Erat historia Rōmae antīquae° longa aut brevis? _____

   Historia Rōmae antīquae erat longa.

   [°ancient] **(Was the history of ancient Rome long or short?)**

5. Estne Ītalia ad Graeciam? _____

   Ītalia est ad Graeciam.

   (Is Italy near Greece?)

6. Estne lingua Germāna similis linguae Anglicae? _____

   Lingua Germāna est similis linguae Anglicae.

   (Is the German language similar to the English language?)

7. Quālis dux erat Julius Caesar? _____

   Julius Caesar erat dux magnus/fortis/audāx.

   (What kind of leader was Julius Caesar?)

© 1999 BJU Press. Reproduction prohibited.

Give a brief Latin answer to each question. Use the gender and case that would be correct in a complete sentence answer.

1. Fortis est Dominus Deus. (from Revelation 18:8)

   Quālis Deus est Dominus? _____ *Fortis* _____

   (The Lord God is strong. / Strong is the Lord God. What kind of God is the Lord?)

2. Tempus Salvātōris nostrī in terrā erat brevis.

   Eratne vīta Christī in terrā longa aut brevis? _____ *brevis* _____

   (The time of our Savior on earth was short. Was the life of Christ on earth long or short?)

3. Timōtheus iuvenis erat amīcus Paulī.

   Cuius° amīcus erat iuvenis Timōtheus? _____ *Paulī* _____

   [°whose] **(Young Timothy was a friend of Paul. Whose friend was young Timothy?)**

4. Christus Matthaeō mandātum dedit°. Responsum Matthaeī erat celere.

   Quis Christō responsum celere dedit? _____ *Matthaeus* _____

   [°gave] **(Christ gave Matthew a command. Matthew's response was quick. Who gave Christ a quick response?)**

5. Vir° prūdēns in tempore illō malō° tacēbit°.

   Quis in tempore illō malō tacēbit? _____ *Vir prūdēns* _____

   [°man; °bad; °will be silent] **(A prudent man will be silent in that bad time. Who will be silent in that bad time?)**

© 1999 BJU Press. Reproduction prohibited.

Write these noun phrases in the Latin cases indicated.

Nominative

1. a good king _____ *rēx bonus* _____

2. a new thing _____ *rēs nova* _____

3. a strong oak tree _____ *quercus fortis* _____

Genitive

4. of a faithful friend _____ *amīcī fidēlis* _____

5. of a sad boy _____ *puerī tristis* _____

6. of an old senator _____ *senātōris veteris* _____

Dative

7. my father _____ *patrī meō* _____

8. a famous leader _____ *ducī clārō* _____

9. a free country _____ *patriae līberae* _____

Accusative

10. a dismal day _____ *diem tristem* _____

11. a short time _____ *breve tempus* _____

12. a great hope _____ *magnam spem* _____

Ablative

13. a swift horse _____ *equō celerī* _____

14. a sharp word _____ *verbō acrī* _____

15. an easy road _____ *viā facilī* _____

© 1999 BJU Press. Reproduction prohibited.

Translate these sentences. You may supply the verb *est,* which is often omitted from a sentence that contains a predicate adjective or a predicate noun. A few new words are not defined for you because the meanings are obvious from the contexts. Write your translations in pencil; then check the word meanings and correct any errors you may have made. (Scripture verses are from the Vulgate, and references often differ in number from the King James Version.)

In two of the items, the word order has been changed to make the translation easier.

1. Ars° longa, vīta brevis. (Hippocrates, translated from the Greek) _____

   Art [is] long, life [is] short.

   [°art]

2. Nēmo° malus° fēlix°. _____

   No one bad [is] happy.

   [°no one; °bad; °happy]

3. Magna est vēritās et praevalet°. _____

   Great is truth and it prevails.

   [°prevail, triumph]

4. Pūra° aqua ā fonte° purō dēfluit°. _____

   From a pure fountain pure water flows down.

   [°pure; °fountain; °flow down]

5. Deus iūdex° iustus° et fortis et patiēns°. (Psalm 7:12) _____

   God [is] a just and strong and patient judge. / God [is] a judge, just and strong and patient.

   [°judge; °just; °patient]

6. Hic est vērus Deus et vīta aeterna. (I John 5:20) _____

   This is the true God and eternal life.

7. Fortis in Dominō (motto of a Christian school, not a sentence) _____

   Strong in the Lord

© 1999 BJU Press. Reproduction prohibited.

Activity L

Translate each sentence.

1. Verbum Deī est vērum. _____

   The Word of God is true.
   _____

2. Vēritās Scriptūrae est aeterna. _____

   The truth of Scripture is eternal.
   _____

3. Cor peccātōris nōn est līberum. _____

   The heart of a sinner is not free.
   _____

4. Lēx Dominī iusta est. _____

   The law of the Lord is just.
   _____

5. Deus noster est vīvus Deus. _____

   Our God is a living God.
   _____

Activity M

Complete each comparison by filling in the blank.

1. Latin adjectives > Latin nouns
   fidēlis : fidēlitās :: fēlīcis : _____ *fēlīcitās*

2. English adjectives > English nouns
   faithful : faithfulness :: happy : _____ *happiness*

3. Latin adjectives > Latin nouns
   iustus: iustitia :: iniustus : _____ *iniustitia*

4. English adjectives > English nouns
   just : justice :: unjust : _____ *injustice*

5. Latin nouns > English nouns
   facilitās : facility :: quālitās : _____ *quality*

6. Latin adjectives > English adjectives
   potentiālis : potential :: iūdiciālis : _____ *judicial*

7. Latin adjectives > English adjectives
   potentis : potent :: patientis : _____ *patient*

8. Latin adjectives > English adjectives
   vastus : vast :: longus : _____ *long*

© 1999 BJU Press. Reproduction prohibited.

Activity N

Complete each comparison.

1. vēritās : verity :: brevitās : _____ *brevity* _____

2. longus : long :: publicus : _____ *public* _____

3. austrālis : austral :: mortālis : _____ *mortal* _____

4. glōria : glory :: histōria : _____ *history* _____

5. facilitās : facility :: gravitās : _____ *gravity* _____

Activity O

Match the Latin phrases with the English translations. Each phrase contains a Latin noun you have probably not seen before. The adjectives will help you figure out the meanings of the nouns. Notice the agreement of the adjectives and nouns in each phrase.

___*E*___ 1. fabula brevis   A. easy work

___*B*___ 2. puella tristis   B. sad girl

___*H*___ 3. vir līber   C. brave soldier

___*A*___ 4. labor facilis   D. young woman

___*C*___ 5. mīles fortis   E. short story

___*I*___ 6. medicīna acris   F. bold action

___*F*___ 7. actiō audāx   G. bad report

___*D*___ 8. fēmina juvenis   H. free man

___*G*___ 9. fāma mala   I. bitter medicine

___*J*___ 10. liber noster   J. our book

© 1999 BJU Press. Reproduction prohibited.

Activity P

This vocabulary review covers words found in Chapters 1-10. In each part, match the Latin words with their meanings. For each Latin word in the second column that is followed by a blank, write an English derivative. Complete the activity without referring to the chapters or to the Vocābulārium. If your teacher permits, you may then check your answers for accuracy, making corrections in a different-colored pencil or ink. **Answers will vary.**

Part 1

_____F_____ 1. with

_____H_____ 2. God

_____E_____ 3. dog

_____A_____ 4. book

_____G_____ 5. farmer, husbandman

_____J_____ 6. friend

_____D_____ 7. easy

_____I_____ 8. lamb

_____C_____ 9. hard

_____B_____ 10. first

A. liber, -brī, *m.* _____library_____

B. prīmus, -a, -um _____primary/primer/prime_____

C. dūrus, -a -um _____durable_____

D. facilis, -e _____facility_____

E. canis, -is, *m.* _____canine_____

F. cum (with abl. case)

G. agricola, -ae, *m.* _____agriculture_____

H. Deus, -ī, *m.* _____deity_____

I. agnus, -ī, *m.*

J. amīcus, -ī, *m.* _____amicable_____

Part 2

_____H_____ 1. law

_____F_____ 2. horse

_____B_____ 3. heart

_____A_____ 4. water

_____G_____ 5. writing instrument

_____E_____ 6. female pupil

_____D_____ 7. lord, master

_____J_____ 8. severe, heavy

_____C_____ 9. light

_____I_____ 10. free

A. aqua, -ae, *f.* _____aqueduct, aquatic_____

B. cor, cordis, *n.* _____cordial_____

C. lūx, lūcis, *f.* _____Lucifer, lucid_____

D. dominus, -ī, *m.* _____dominion, dominate_____

E. discipula, -ae, *f.* _____disciple_____

F. equus, -ī, *m.* _____equine_____

G. stilus, -ī, *m.* _____stylus_____

H. lēx, lēgis, *f.* _____legal_____

I. līber, -era, -erum _____liberty_____

J. gravis, -e _____gravity_____

© 1999 BJU Press. Reproduction prohibited.

Capitulum 10

CAPITULUM XI

As you read these statements and the questions about them, try to answer the questions without translating. Write short answers in Latin. Put nouns in the case they would be if the answer were a complete sentence. Number 4 has a new word; the meaning should be clear from the context.

1. Deus Christiānōs curat. Quis Christiānōs cūrat? _____ *Deus* _____

   (God cares for Christians. Who cares for Christians?)

2. Christus peccātōrēs invenit et servat. Quis peccātōrēs invenit et servat? _____ *Christus* _____

   (Christ finds and saves sinners. Who finds and saves sinners?)

3. Salvātor peccātōrī magnam spem dat. Quid Salvātor peccātōrī dat? _____ *magnam spem* _____

   (The Savior gives great hope to the sinner. What does the Savior give to the sinner?)

4. Peccātōrēs salvātiōnem in Christō inveniunt. Quid peccātōrēs in Christō inveniunt?

   _____ *salvātiōnem / salvātiōnem in Christō* _____

   (Sinners find salvation in Christ. What do sinners find in Christ?)

5. Peccātōrēs in Christō veniam et pācem quoque° inveniunt. Quī° veniam et pācem

   inveniunt in Christō? _____ *peccātōrēs* _____

   [°also; °who (plural)] **(Sinners also find forgiveness and peace in Christ. Who find forgiveness and peace in Christ?)**

6. Christiānī salvātiōnem, veniam, et pācem in Christō habent. Quī salvātiōnem, veniam

   et pācem habent in Christō? _____ *Christiānī* _____

   (Christians have salvation, forgiveness, and peace in Christ. Who have salvation, forgiveness, and peace in Christ?)

© 1999 BJU Press. Reproduction prohibited.

Write these noun phrases in Latin, being careful to use the correct inflections.

1. the king's daughters (subject) _____ *fīliae rēgis* _____
2. a long river (direct object) _____ *longum flūmen* _____
3. long rivers (direct object) _____ *longa flūmina* _____
4. strong young men (subject) _____ *iuvenēs fortēs* _____
5. strong young men (direct object) _____ *iuvenēs fortēs* _____
6. happy boys (subject) _____ *puerī fēlīcēs* _____
7. small twins (direct object) _____ *parvōs geminōs* _____
8. a friendly dog (subject) _____ *canis amīcus* _____
9. faithful friends (subject) _____ *amīcī fidēlēs* _____
10. faithful friends (direct object) _____ *amīcōs fidēlēs* _____

Activity C

Write these phrases in Latin. Use the correct case—ablative or accusative—after each preposition.

1. across the river _____ *trāns flūmen* _____
2. with a twin _____ *cum geminō* _____
3. toward Remus's brother _____ *ad frātrem Remī* _____
4. with a woodpecker _____ *cum pīcō* _____
5. mother of Romulus and Remus _____ *māter Rōmulī et Remī* _____
6. son and daughter of the king (subject) _____ *fīlius et fīlia rēgis* _____
7. happy daughters (subject) _____ *fīliae fēlīcēs* _____
8. happy sons (direct object) _____ *fīliōs fēlīcēs* _____
9. strong wall (subject) _____ *mūrus fortis* _____
10. strong kingdom (subject) _____ *regnum forte* _____
11. great kingdoms (direct object) _____ *magna regna / regna magna* _____
12. friendly young men (direct object) _____ *iuvenēs amīcōs* _____

© 1999 BJU Press. Reproduction prohibited.

Activity D

Write each sentence in Latin. Be careful to use the correct case endings for nouns and adjectives and to use *-nt* for plural verbs.

1. Numitor is Amulius's brother. _____

   Numitor est frāter Amūlī/Amūliī.

2. Numitor's brother is bad. _____

   Frāter Numitōris est malus.

3. Rhea Silvia has twins. _____

   Rhea Silvia geminōs habet.

4. The boys do not find death in the river Tiber. _____

   Puerī mortem in flūmine Tibere nōn inveniunt.

5. Amulius is not the new king of Alba Longa. _____

   Amūlius nōn est rēx novus Albae Longae.

Activity E

Answer each question in a complete Latin sentence. Base your answers on the Romulus and Remus story.

1. Estne māter Rōmulī et Remī fīlia Numitōris aut Amūlī? _____

   Māter Rōmulī et Remī est fīlia Numitōris.

   (Is the mother of Romulus and Remus the daughter of Numitor or Amulius?)

2. Cuius regnum Amūlius capit? _____

   Amūlius regnum Numitōris capit.

   (Whose kingdom does Amulius seize?)

3. Quōrum mortem Amūlius intendit? _____

   Amūlius mortem Rōmulī et Remī / geminōrum / puerōrum intendit.

   (Whose death does Amulius plan?)

4. Quōrum cūra° vītās geminōrum servat? _____

   Cūra lupī et pīcī vītās geminōrum servat.

   [°care] **(Whose care saves the lives of the twins?)**

5. Quōrum pater est deus Mars in fabulā? _____

   In fabulā deus Mars est pater Rōmulī et Remī / geminōrum / puerōrum.

   (Whose father is the god Mars in the story?)

© 1999 BJU Press. Reproduction prohibited.

From what you learned by reading Parts I and II of "Rōmulus et Remus," give brief Latin answers to these questions. Use the noun inflections you would use in sentence answers.

1. Quōrum pater est Numitor? _____ *Rōmulī et Remī / geminōrum / puerōrum* _____

   (Whose father is Numitor?)

2. Cuius frāter est rēx Albae Longae? _____ *Amūlī/Amūliī* _____

   (Whose brother is the king of Alba Longa?)

3. Cuius frāter est malus? _____ *Numitōris* _____

   (Whose brother is bad?)

4. Quōrum vītās lupus et pīcus servant? _____ *Rōmulī et Remī / geminōrum / puerōrum* _____

   (Whose lives do the wolf and the woodpecker save?)

5. Eratne Rōma prīmō urbs aut oppidum? _____ *oppidum* _____

   (Was Rome at first / At first was Rome a city or a town?)

© 1999 BJU Press. Reproduction prohibited.

Answer each question in Latin. Your answers may be brief. The pronouns *quis* and *quem* are singular in number.

1. Quōrum mater est Rhea Silvia? _____ *Rōmulī et Remī / geminōrum / puerōrum* _____

   (Whose mother is Rhea Silvia?)

2. Quis geminōs invenit et cūrat? _____ *pastor* _____

   (Who finds and cares for the twins?)

3. Quis est malus? _____ *Amūlius* _____

   (Who is bad?)

4. Quōrum vītās pastor servat? _____ *Rōmulī et Remī / geminōrum / puerōrum* _____

   (Whose lives does the shepherd save?)

5. Quem iuvenēs necant? _____ *Amūlium* _____

   (Whom do the young men kill?)

6. Quid condunt? _____ *oppidum* _____

   (What do they establish?)

7. Quid Rōmulus construit? _____ *mūrum circum oppidum* _____

   (What does Romulus construct?)

8. Quis ridet? _____ *Remus* _____

   (Who laughs?)

9. Quis quem necat? _____ *Rōmulus Remum necat* _____

   (Who kills whom?)

10. Quis est rēx prīmus Rōmae? _____ *Rōmulus* _____

    (Who is the first king of Rome?)

© 1999 BJU Press. Reproduction prohibited.

Fill in the first blank with the letter of a correct translation from the last column. Then decide what function(s) each phrase can have in a Latin sentence. In the second blank add the correct abbreviation(s) to show possible function(s) of the phrase. (The adjective *memor* means "thoughtful.")

Use these abbreviations:

S (subject)   IO (indirect object)

Poss (possessive)   DO (direct object)

                                             OP (object of a preposition)

E	S	1. mūrus fortis	A. of large kingdoms
C	Poss	2. parvōrum geminōrum	B. easy remedy
G	Poss	3. flūminum longōrum	C. of the small twins
A	Poss	4. magnōrum regnōrum	D. for your son
I	S, DO	5. iuvenēs fēlīcēs	E. strong wall
F	Poss, S	6. fīliae nostrae	F. of our daughter
D	IO, OP	7. fīliō tuō	G. of long rivers
H	S	8. frāter memor	H. thoughtful brother
J	DO	9. mātrēs nostrās	I. happy young men
B	DO, OP	10. remedium facile	J. our mothers

Complete each sentence by filling in the blank(s). After you complete the sentences, check your answers with the section called "Roman Kings and the Early Roman Republic."

1. Rome was built on _____ seven _____ hills.

2. Rome had _____ seven _____ kings.

3. The name of the first king was _____ Romulus _____, and the name of the last king was _____ Tarquin _____ the Proud.

4. The kingdom lasted from _____ 753 _____ B.C. to _____ 509 _____ B.C.

5. The last king was banished because of his crimes. He went to live with the _____ Etruscans _____.

6. Rome then became a republic. The government was headed by two men of equal authority. They were called _____ consuls _____.

© 1999 BJU Press. Reproduction prohibited.

In the first blank, write the Latin word that is suggested by the underlined word in each sentence. In the second blank, write the meaning of the Latin word. In number 10 the derivative consists of a prefix and a Latin noun.

1. The <u>curator</u> was careful in his handling of all the items in the museum.

   cūrat   *cares for*

2. Most of us accomplish less in a day than we <u>intend</u>.

   intendit   *plans*

3. The <u>conservation</u> of natural resources is one of the functions of the federal government. *servat*   *saves*

4. The invading army plans to <u>capture</u> that town.

   capit   *takes*

5. Our Latin vocabulary is <u>increasing</u> with every chapter.

   crescit   *grows*

6. <u>Inventors</u> find easier ways to do things.

   invenit   *finds*

7. We can often <u>evade</u> problems by careful thinking.

   ēvādit   *escapes*

8. Some <u>juvenile</u> behavior needs correction.

   iuvenis   *a young person*

9. The water flowing through the <u>flume</u> was clear and pure.

   flūmen   *river*

10. For many centuries England has been ruled by kings or queens, but for a brief <u>interregnum</u> a "lord protector" and parliament governed without a king.

    regnum   *kingdom*

© 1999 BJU Press. Reproduction prohibited.

The first column contains English adjectives made from nouns you have worked with. Match these adjectives with their basic definitions. You may need to look back to earlier chapters for the Latin origins of some of these words.

_C_	1. arboreal	A.	pertaining to a remedy
_G_	2. imperial	B.	pertaining to a teacher or master
_B_	3. magisterial	C.	pertaining to a tree
_J_	4. mural	D.	pertaining to a word
_F_	5. pastoral	E.	pertaining to death
_A_	6. remedial	F.	pertaining to a shepherd
_E_	7. mortal	G.	pertaining to an empire or to power
_K_	8. real	H.	pertaining to war
_D_	9. verbal	I.	pertaining to life
_I_	10. vital	J.	pertaining to a wall
_H_	11. martial	K.	pertaining to a thing

Based on your knowledge of Latin word meanings, fill in each blank with an English word that completes the thought.

1. A <u>crescendo</u> in music indicates an ___*increase*___ in sound volume.

2. A <u>mortal</u> wound is a wound that results in ___*death*___.

3. In a <u>fraternal</u> organization, the members treat each other like ___*brothers*___.

4. A person's <u>maternal</u> grandmother is his grandmother on his ___*mother's*___ side of the family.

5. A <u>judicial</u> decision is a decision made by a ___*judge*___.

6. <u>Juvenile</u> behavior is the behavior of a typical ___*young*___ person.

7. A person who <u>ridicules</u> another is one who ___*laughs*___ at the other person.

© 1999 BJU Press. Reproduction prohibited.

Follow the general pattern of making English adjectives from Latin adjectives that came from Latin nouns. Write the English adjective.

1. pastor > pastorālis > _____ *pastoral* _____

2. virtūs > virtuālis > _____ *virtual* _____

3. imperium > imperiālis > _____ *imperial* _____

4. mūrus > mūrālis > _____ *mural* _____

5. spiritus > spirituālis > _____ *spiritual* _____

© 1999 BJU Press. Reproduction prohibited.

CAPITULUM XII

© 1999 BJU Press. Reproduction prohibited.

Activity A

In each blank write *A* for a person or group that belonged to the patrician class or *B* for a member or members of the plebian class. If both patricians and plebians are referred to, write *C*.

___C___ 1. discussed in Livy's history of Rome

___C___ 2. tribunes

___A___ 3. senators

___A___ 4. about ten percent of the Romans

___B___ 5. majority of Romans

___A___ 6. noblemen

___C___ 7. included in SPQR

Activity B

Match the Latin words and phrases with their translations by writing the letter of the translation in the blank. Most of the nouns are plural; a few are singular. One translation will not be used.

___C___ 1. puerīs

___H___ 2. rēgum

___J___ 3. puerī currunt

___F___ 4. iuvenibus

___I___ 5. grātia fīliārum

___A___ 6. amīcus senātōribus

___G___ 7. flūmina aquārum

___L___ 8. similis quercibus

___B___ 9. opus senātūs

___E___ 10. victōria plēbis

___K___ 11. cum geminīs

A. friendly to the senators

B. the work of the senate

C. for the boys

D. the name of the king

E. the victory of the common people

F. for the young men

G. rivers of waters

H. of kings

I. gratitude of the daughters

J. boys are running

K. with the twins

L. similar to oak trees

After reading each sentence, answer in Latin the question that follows. Your answers need not be complete sentences, but be sure that all nouns and adjectives that you write are in the case they would be if you wrote a whole sentence. *Populus* is singular in form even though it refers to more than one person.

1. Tarquinius Superbus populō multa iūra nōn dedit°.

    Cui multa iura Tarquinius Superbus nōn dedit? _____ *Populō*

    [°gave] **(Tarquin the Proud did not give the people many rights. To whom did Tarquin the Proud not give many rights?)**

2. Senātōribus magnam honōrem Rōma dedit.

    Quibus magnam honōrem Rōma dedit? _____ *Senātōribus*

    (Rome gave great honor to the senators. To whom did Rome give great honor?)

3. Historia iuvenibus vītās magnōrum ducum ostendit.

    Quibus vītās magnōrum ducum historia ostendit? _____ *Iuvenibus*

    (History shows young men / people the lives of great leaders. To whom does history show the lives of great leaders?)

4. Līvius Rōmae historiam urbis et reī publicae dedit.

    Cui Līvius historiam urbis et reī publicae dedit? _____ *Rōmae*

    (Livy gave Rome a history of the city and the republic. To whom did Livy give a history of the city and the republic?)

5. Ad fīnem° reī publicae Rōmānae, Cicero senātuī multās ōrātiōnēs dedit.

    Cui Cicero multās ōrātiōnēs dedit? _____ *Senātuī*

    [°end] **(Near/At the end of the Roman republic, Cicero gave many speeches to the senate. To whom did Cicero give many speeches?)**

© 1999 BJU Press. Reproduction prohibited.

© 1999 BJU Press. Reproduction prohibited.

Activity D

Read each sentence and then answer the question in Latin without going through the translation process. Make your answers complete sentences. Both the Latin noun *plebs* and the English loan word *plebs* are collective nouns and take singular verbs.

1. Coriolānus tribūnīs plēbis nōn est amīcus.

   Dīligitne Coriolānus tribūnōs plēbis? _____

   _____ **Coriolānus tribūnōs plēbis nōn dīligit.** _____

   (Coriolanus is not friendly to the tribunes of the plebs. Does Coriolānus love the tribunes of the plebs?)

2. Plebs Coriolānō inimīca est.

   Quis est inimīca Coriolānō? _____

   _____ **Plebs est inimīca Coriolānō.** _____

   (The plebs is unfriendly/hostile to Coriolanus. Who is unfriendly to Coriolanus?)

3. Plebs tribūnīs est amīca.

   Quibus est plebs amīca? _____

   _____ **Tribūnīs plebs est amīca.** _____

   (The plebs is friendly to the tribunes. To whom is the plebs friendly?)

4. Plebs Coriolānō honōrem nōn dat.

   Datne plebs Coriolānō honōrem? _____

   _____ **Plebs Coriolānō honōrem nōn dat.** _____

   (The plebs does not give Coriolanus honor. Does the plebs give Coriolanus honor?)

5. Patriciī ūnō ducī, nōn multīs ducibus, nōmen Coriolānī dant.

   Dantne patriciī multīs ducibus nōmen Coriolānī? _____

   _____ **Patriciī ūnō ducī, nōn multīs ducibus, nōmen Coriolānī dant.** _____

   (The patricians give to one leader, not to many leaders, the name of Coriolanus. Do the patricians give to many leaders the name of Coriolanus?)

Written exercises 91

Without translating what you have just read, write brief answers to these questions. Be sure the case of any nouns in your answers is the correct case you would use in a complete sentence answer.

1. Estne Gnaeus Marcius dux patricius aut dux plēbēius? _____*Dux patricius*_____

    (Is Gnaeus Marcius a patrician leader or a plebian leader?)

2. Quis exercitum Rōmānum contrā oppidum Coriolōrum ducit? _____*Gnaeus Marcius*_____

    (Who leads the Roman army against the town of Corioli?)

3. Vincitne dux Rōmānus oppidum Coriolōrum? _____*Ita vērē / Vincit / Ita vērē vincit*_____

    (Does the Roman leader conquer the town of Corioli?)

4. Quid est nōmen novum° Gnaeī Marcī? _____*Coriolānus*_____

    [°new] **(What is the new name of Gnaeus Marcius? / What is Gnaeus Marcius's new name?)**

5. Quibus est Coriolānus inimīcus? _____*Tribūnīs plēbis*_____

    (To whom is Coriolanus unfriendly/hostile?)

6. Cui est plebs Rōmāna inimīca? _____*Coriolānō*_____

    (To whom is the Roman plebs unfriendly/hostile?)

7. Quis dēnique est inimīcus Rōmae? _____*Coriolānus*_____

    (Who finally is unfriendly/hostile to Rome?)

© 1999 BJU Press. Reproduction prohibited.

© 1999 BJU Press. Reproduction prohibited.

Activity F

Base your Latin answers to these questions on the Latin paragraphs you just read. You may give brief answers, but be sure to use the noun and adjective endings that would be correct if you gave sentence answers.

1. Quis est in historiā fābulāque? _____ *Cincinnātus* _____

   (Who is in history and legend?)

2. Quis contrā Aequōs pugnat? _____ *Exercitus Rōmānus* _____

   (Who is fighting / fights against the Aequians?)

3. Superantne Rōmānī Aequōs? _____ *Nōn superant* _____

   (Do the Romans overcome the Aequians?)

4. Quem ducēs Rōmānī vocant? _____ *Cincinnātum* _____

   (Whom do the Roman leaders/generals call?)

5. Ubī° est agricola? _____ *In agrō* _____

   [°where] **(Where is the farmer?)**

6. Cui Rōmānī ducēs titulum dictātōris dant? _____ *Cincinnātō* _____

   (To whom do the Roman leaders give the title of dictator?)

7. Quibus Rōmānī magnam clādem dant? _____ *Aequīs* _____

   (To whom do the Romans give a great defeat?)

8. Quis exercitum Rōmānum ad victōriam dūcit? _____ *Cincinnātus* _____

   (Who leads the Roman army to victory?)

9. Tum ubī Cincinnātus redit? _____ *Ad agrum* _____

   (Then where does Cincinnatus go back?)

(1) Label the case of each noun and (2) translate each sentence. Look in the Vocābulārium for the meaning of *grex* that is correct in the context of number 4. Check the list earlier in this chapter or the Vocābulārium for the meanings of any other words you are not sure of. Take time now to learn any words you have to look up.

Use these abbreviations for the case names: *N* (nominative), *G* (genitive), *D* (dative), *Acc* (accusative), *Abl* (ablative).

        N   *Acc*
1. Tribūnus multōs equōs habet. _____

           The tribune has many horses.

      N   *Acc*   *G*
2. Agricola equōs tribūnī cūrat. _____

         The/A farmer cares for the tribune's horses / the horses of the tribune.

     D   *Acc*   *Acc*
3. Equīs cibum° et aquam dat. _____

         He gives food and water to the horses / the horses food and water.

[°food]

     N   *G*
4. Grex equōrum est magnus. _____

         The herd of horses is large.

     N   *Abl*
5. Equī celerēs in viā currunt. _____

         The swift horses run / are running in / on the road.

     N   *G*   *D*
6. Tribūnus plēbis est amīcus agricolīs. _____

        The tribune of the common people / plebs is friendly to the farmers.

     N   *G*   *Acc*
7. Ducēs exercituum equōs bonōs habent. _____

         Leaders/Generals of armies have good horses.

    N   *N*   *D*   *A*
8. Rēgēs et ducēs rēbus multīs° tempus dant. _____

        Kings and generals give time to many things/affairs.

[°many]

     N   *G*   *G*
9. Opus rēgum et senātōrum nōn est facile. _____

        The work of kings and senators is not easy.

     N   *Acc* *G*
10. Rēgēs bonī iura cīvium dēfendunt. _____

        Good kings defend the rights of citizens.

© 1999 BJU Press. Reproduction prohibited.

© 1999 BJU Press. Reproduction prohibited.

Activity H

These sentences from ancient Latin writings contain plural nouns in the dative case. Two of the sentences were revised slightly to make translation easier. Write the translation of each sentence.

For words having meanings that are obvious because of their closeness to related English words, the meanings are not given.

1. Vīta mortālibus nihil° sine magnō labōre dat. _____

   Life gives mortals / to mortals nothing without great labor.

   [°nothing]

2. Carmina° nova puellīs° et puerīs cantō°. _____

   I sing new songs for/to girls and boys.

   [°songs; °girls; °sing]

3. Populus stultus° virīs° indignīs° honōrēs saepe° dat. _____

   The/A foolish people often gives unworthy men honors.

   [°foolish; °men; °unworthy; °often]

4. Magistrī puerīs parvīs crustula° saepe dant. _____

   Teachers often give small boys cookies / cookies to small boys.

   [°cookies]

Activity I

Match each word in column 2 with the phrase in column 1 that defines or explains it. The meanings of related Latin words are your clues to correct matches. If necessary, you may refer to the list of vocabulary words in the Essential Information for this lesson.

Beside the word in column 2, write the Latin word that clarifies the match.

_C_ 1. eager to fight	A. vocation	*vocat*
_E_ 2. something new or strange	B. contradict	*contrā/dīcit*
_J_ 3. on the winning side	C. pugnacious	*pugnat*
_G_ 4. pertaining to cultivating fields	D. unify	*unus*
_H_ 5. seeming to be every<u>where</u> at once	E. novelty	*novus*
_D_ 6. to make into a unit	F. plebian	*plebs/plēbius*
_A_ 7. a person's calling	G. agrarian	*ager*
_I_ 8. not friendly	H. ubiquitous	*ubī*
_F_ 9. pertaining to the common people	I. inimical	*inimīcus*
_B_ 10. to speak against	J. victorious	*victōria*

Written exercises

Activity J

You have now been introduced formally or informally to hundreds of words. In this review, you are to match opposites.

In each space, write the letter for the word in column 2 that is opposite in meaning.

_____F_____ 1. ante   A. parvus, -a, -um

_____H_____ 2. cum   B. mors, mortis

_____J_____ 3. ā, ab   C. stat

_____D_____ 4. brevis, -e   D. longus, -a, -um

_____G_____ 5. bonus, -a, -um   E. inimīcus, -a, -um

_____I_____ 6. discit   F. post

_____E_____ 7. amīcus, -a, -um   G. malus, -a, -um

_____C_____ 8. iacet   H. sine

_____A_____ 9. magnus, -a, -um   I. docet

_____B_____10. vīta, -ae   J. ad

Activity K

Another way to remember Latin words is to group them according to meaning. Match with their meanings these Latin adjectives that can describe a character trait or an emotion.

_____J_____ 1. amīcus, -a, -um   A. strong

_____E_____ 2. audāx, audācis   B. unjust

_____H_____ 3. fēlix, -līcis   C. faithful

_____C_____ 4. fidēlis, -e   D. powerful

_____A_____ 5. fortis, -e   E. bold

_____B_____ 6. iniustus, -a, -um   F. patient

_____I_____ 7. iustus, -a, -um   G. sad

_____G_____ 8. tristis, -e   H. happy

_____F_____ 9. patiēns, -ientis   I. just

_____D_____10. potēns, -entis   J. friendly

© 1999 BJU Press. Reproduction prohibited.

CAPITULUM XIII

© 1999 BJU Press. Reproduction prohibited.

Activity A

Fill in each blank with the appropriate noun.

1. Pater patrī meī est _____*avus*_____ meus.

   (My father's father / The father of my father is my grandfather.)

2. Māter patrī meī est _____*avia*_____ mea.

   (My father's mother / The mother of my father is my grandmother.)

3. Fīlia parentium meōrum est _____*soror*_____ mea.

   (My parents' daughter / The daughter of my parents is my sister.)

4. Parentēs parentium meōrum sunt _____*aviae*_____ meae et _____*avī*_____ meī.

   (My parents' parents / The parents of my parents are my grandmothers and my grandfathers.)

5. Fīlius avī meī est patruus° meus aut _____*pater*_____ meus.

   [°uncle] **(A son of my grandfather is my uncle or my father.)**

6. Frātrēs meī, sorōrēs meae, et ego _____*patrī nostrō / patrī familiae nostrae*_____ et

   _____*matrī nostrae / mātrī familiae nostrae*_____ honōrem dant.

   (My brothers, my sisters, and I give honor to our father / the father of our family and to our mother / the mother of our family.)

Activity B

Write the English derivative that comes most directly from the Latin word given.

1. aeternitās: _____*eternity*_____

2. antīquitās: _____*antiquity*_____

3. celeritās: _____*celerity*_____

4. clāritās: _____*clarity*_____

5. facilitās: _____*facility*_____

6. fēlīcitās: _____*felicity*_____

7. fīdēlitās: _____*fidelity*_____

8. lībertās: _____*liberty*_____

9. vēritās: _____*verity*_____

Activity C

Write the English derivative that comes directly from the Latin adjective. A helpful clue is given in parentheses. Some of these clues are adjectives from Late Latin or Medieval Latin.

When a word containing a Latin diphthong, such as *ae,* is borrowed into English, one of the vowels is usually dropped.

1. aeternus, -a, -um (aeternālis, -e) _____ *eternal*

2. iūdex, -icis (jūdiciālis, -e) _____ *judicial*

3. līber, -bera, -berum (līberālis, -e) _____ *liberal*

4. manus, -ūs, *f.* (manuālis, -e) _____ *manual*

5. prīmus, -a, -um (prīmālis, -e) _____ *primal*

6. rēs, reī, *f.* (reālis, -e) _____ *real*

7. tempus, temporis, *n.* (temporālis, -e) _____ *temporal*

8. verbum, -ī, *n.* (verbālis, -e) _____ *verbal*

9. vīta, -ae, *f.* (vītālis, -e) _____ *vital*

Activity D

You have seen that many derivatives come into English in groups, following common patterns. This activity serves two purposes: (1) it reviews vocabulary from earlier lessons, and (2) it can add to your understanding of English words as you see how they came from their Latin origins.

Complete each comparison by filling in the appropriate English word. The first part of the comparison shows you how to form the second part.

1. Germānus : German :: Christiānus : _____ *Christian*

2. iūstus : just :: publicus : _____ *public*

3. Troiānus : Trojan :: spiritus : _____ *spirit*

4. truncus : trunk :: porcus : _____ *pork*

5. vastus : vast :: longus : _____ *long*

6. prīmus : prime :: pūrus : _____ *pure*

7. sōlus : sole :: secūrus : _____ *secure*

8. tribūnus : tribune :: senātus : _____ *senate*

9. historia : history :: glōria : _____ *glory*

10. victōria : victory :: Trōia : _____ *Troy*

11. Rōma : Rome :: Eurōpa : _____ *Europe*

12. Vulgāta : Vulgate :: Scriptūra : _____ *Scripture*

© 1999 BJU Press. Reproduction prohibited.

Capitulum 13

Write these phrases in Latin.

1. with Marcus's parents _____ *cum parentibus Marcī* _____

2. among the sisters and brothers _____ *in sorōribus et frātrīs* _____

3. sons and daughters in Roman schools _____ *fīliī et fīliae in scholīs Rōmānīs* _____

4. a book about the sisters and brothers of a famous Roman leader _____
   liber dē sorōribus et frātribus ducis clārī Rōmānī _____

5. from fathers and mothers _____ *ē/ex/ā/ab/dē patribus et matribus* _____

6. with wives and children _____ *cum uxōribus et līberīs* _____

7. concerning grandfathers, grandmothers, and grandchildren _____
   dē avīs, avīīs, et nepōtibus _____

8. from boys and girls _____ *ē/ex/ā/ab/dē puerīs et puellīs* _____

9. concerning the men and women in Rome _____
   dē virīs et mulieribus/fēminīs in Rōmā _____

Translate these sentences.

1. Pater et māter Quintī et Atticī in Ītaliā vivunt. _____
   The father and mother of Quintus and Atticus live in Italy. _____

2. Parentēs puerōrum fīliīs suīs° equōs dant. _____
   The boys' parents give their sons horses / horses to their sons. _____
   [°their]

3. Equī sunt in agrīs. _____
   The horses are in the fields. _____

4. Sub quercibus stant. _____
   They stand / are standing under the oak trees. _____

5. Fulvia et Carolus sunt soror et frāter, līberī parentium clarōrum. _____
   Fulvia and Carolus are sister and brother, children of famous parents. _____

6. Parentibus suīs honōrem ostendunt. _____
   They show honor to their parents / their parents honor. _____

© 1999 BJU Press. Reproduction prohibited.

7. Parentēs magnās spēs dē līberīs suīs habent. _____

The parents have great hopes concerning their children.

8. Paterfamilias Rōmānus multum opus dē rēbus familiae facit°. _____

The Roman father of the family does much work concerning the affairs of the family.

[°does]

Activity G

Write the letter for each matching English phrase. Ignore the underlining. It pertains to Activity H.

I 1. uxōrī Cincinnātī	A. the names of the friendly women
H 2. nōmina geminōrum	B. with Caesar's nephew
L 3. avus Rōmulī Remīque	C. concerning Brutus's parents
J 4. māter Coriolānī	D. in the days of the kings
B 5. cum nepōte Caesaris	E. without brothers and sisters
C 6. dē parentibus Brūtī	F. for boys and girls
D 7. in diēbus rēgum	G. the grandmother of Caesar
A 8. nōmina fēminārum amīcārum	H. the twins' names
F 9. puerīs puellīsque	I. for the wife of Cincinnatus
E 10. sine fratribus et sorōribus	J. Coriolanus's mother
K 11. fabula dē familiā in Etrūriā	K. the legend about a family in Etruria
	L. Romulus's and Remus's grand-father / the grandfather of Romulus and Remus

© 1999 BJU Press. Reproduction prohibited.

Activity H

Copy each underlined noun in Activity G and write its case name in the blank. Determine the case of the noun from the context. Do not abbreviate the case names and be sure to spell each case correctly.

1. *uxōrī* — *dative*
2. *geminōrum* — *genitive*
3. *avus* — *nominative*
4. *Coriolānī* — *genitive*
5. *nepōte* — *ablative*
6. *parentibus* — *ablative*
7. *rēgum* — *genitive*
8. *fēminārum* — *genitive*
9. *puerīs* — *dative*
10. *sorōribus* — *ablative*
11. *familiā* — *ablative*

Activity I

Write each phrase in Latin. If necessary, you may check the Vocābulārium for the genders of the nouns.

1. of many skills — *multārum artium*
2. of little cats — *parvārum fēlium*
3. of many infants — *multōrum/multārum infantium*
4. large animals (direct object) — *magna animalia*
5. of large bridges — *magnōrum pontium*

Activity J

Write each phrase in English. Remember that an adjective showing size or number usually precedes the noun it modifies.

1. omnēs vītae — *all lives*
2. multa tempora — *many times*
3. multae fābulae — *many stories/legends/fables*
4. brevēs librī — *short books*
5. ōrātiōnēs similēs — *similar orations*
6. puellae tristēs — *sad girls*

© 1999 BJU Press. Reproduction prohibited.

7. remedia facilia _____ *easy remedies* _____

8. vastōrum montium _____ *of vast mountains* _____

9. cum frātribus meīs _____ *with my brothers* _____

10. equōs celerēs _____ *swift horses* _____

11. virīs fortibus (indirect object) _____ *to/for strong men* _____

12. cum amīcīs fidēlibus _____ *with faithful friends* _____

Activity K

Translate these statements made by Romans. For some, the writer is not known. Each contains a noun (singular or plural) modified by an adjective. Some of the words that are new to you are so much like English derivatives that you need not be told their meanings.

1. Omnis ars imitātiō natūrae est. (Seneca) _____

   _____ *All art is an imitation of nature.* _____

2. Vir bonus es°. (Terence) _____

   _____ *You are a good man.* _____

   [°you are]

3. Vīta mortālibus° nil° sine magnō labōre dedit. (Horace's word order: Nil sine magnō vīta labōre dedit mortālibus.) _____

   _____ *Life has given / gave nothing to mortals without great labor.* _____

   [°mortals; °nothing]

4. Dīvīna natūra dedit agrōs; ars hūmāna aedificāvit° urbēs. _____

   _____ *Divine nature gave the fields; human skill/art built the cities.* _____

   [°built]

5. Vīta hominis brevis est. _____

   _____ *The life of man / a man's life is short.* _____

6. Mortālia omnia mūtātiōnēs° multās habent. _____

   _____ *All mortal things have many changes.* _____

   [°change]

7. Mors est inevitabilis. _____

   _____ *Death is inevitable.* _____

8. Multī cīvēs° perīcula° nōn vident. (Cicero) _____

   _____ *Many citizens do not see dangers.* _____

   [°citizen; °danger]

© 1999 BJU Press. Reproduction prohibited.

© 1999 BJU Press. Reproduction prohibited.

Activity L

Write the underlined phrases in Latin. Remember that adjectives must agree with the nouns they modify in gender, number, and case. They agree in declension only if the adjective and the noun are in the same declension.

1. Horatius was a hero in the Roman army.

    in exercitū Rōmānō

2. Under the leadership of Horatius, the Romans fought the Etruscan soldiers.

    mīlitēs Etruscōs

3. With the help of good friends, Horatius stopped the Etruscans.

    amīcōrum bonōrum

4. All the boys and girls feared the Etruscans.

    Omnēs puerī et puellae

5. With brave friends Horatius kept the Etruscans away from Rome.

    Cum amīcīs fortibus

6. Horatius and his friends brought Roman men and women safety.

    virīs et fēminīs Rōmānīs

Activity M

Answer these questions in Latin. Most of your answers can be brief. In brief answers be sure that nouns are in the case that would be needed if the answers were complete sentences.

1. Quī° stant ad pontem? _____ *Rōmānī/Omnēs (virī, fēminae, puerī, puellae)*

    [°who] **(Who are standing at the bridge?)**

2. Quī exercitum Etruscōrum timent? _____ *Omnēs Rōmānī / Omnēs—virī, fēminae, puerī, [et] puellae*

    (Who fear the army of the Etruscans?)

3. Quālis exercitus est exercitus Etruscus? _____ *Fortis / Fortis exercitus*

    (What kind of army is the Etruscan army?)

4. Ubi est exercitus Etruscus? _____ *Trāns flūmen*

    (Where is the Etruscan army?)

5. Ubi est Horātius? _____ *In ponte (super flūmine Tibere)*

    (Where is Horatius?)

6. Qui sunt cum Horātiō? _____ *Duo amīcī*

    (Who are with Horatius?)

7. Quis Etruscōs pugnat et qui pontem siccīdunt? *Horātius (sōlus). Duo amīcī Horātī/Horātiī*

   (Who fights the Etruscans and who cut down the bridge?)

8. Natantne ad terram Horātius et amīcī duo suī? *Ita vērē. Ad terram natant.*

   (Do Horatius and his two friends swim to land?)

9. Caditne tōtus pōns in flūmen? *Ita vērē. (Tōtus pōns cadit in flūmen.)*

   (Does the whole bridge fall into the river?)

10. Cūr° est Rōma secūra? *Sine ponte Etruscī nullam viam ad Rōmam habent.*

    [°why] **(Why is Rome safe?)**

Activity N

Write **T** or **F** to indicate whether the statement is true or false. Base your answers on the content of the paragraphs entitled "Horatius ad Pontem."

_____T_____ 1. Exercitus Etruscus est trāns flūmen Tiberim ab cīvibus Rōmānīs.

   (The Etruscan army is across the river Tiber from the Roman citizens.)

_____F_____ 2. Virī in exercitū Etruscōrum familiās Rōmānōrum timent.

   (The men in the army of the Etruscans fear the families of the Romans.)

_____T_____ 3. Pōns super flūmen Tiberim est via ab exercitū Etruscō ad Rōmam.

   (The bridge over the river Tiber is the way from the Etruscan army to Rome.)

_____T_____ 4. Horātius et duo amīcī sunt fortēs.

   (Horatius and two friends are brave/strong.)

_____F_____ 5. Etruscī trāns pontem in Rōmam veniunt.

   (The Etruscans come across the bridge into Rome.)

_____T_____ 6. Horātius solus pugnat in ponte.

   (Horatius alone fights on the bridge.)

_____T_____ 7. Pōns in flūmen Tiberim cadit.

   (The bridge falls into the river Tiber.)

_____T_____ 8. Duo amīcī Horātī ad terram natant.

   (Horatius's two friends swim to the land.)

_____F_____ 9. Exercitus Rōmānus exercitum Etruscum pugnat.

   (The Roman army fights the Etruscan army.)

_____T_____ 10. Horātius Rōmam servat. Rōma Horātium dīligit.

   (Horatius saves Rome. Rome loves Horatius.)

© 1999 BJU Press. Reproduction prohibited.

Translate the Latin portions of these verses. Then use your Bible to check the accuracy of your translation and the spelling of proper nouns. (Some punctuation and wording in the King James Version differs slightly from what we usually use today.)

1. [And every one that hath forsaken houses, or] frātrēs aut sorōrēs aut patrem aut matrem aut uxōrem aut fīliōs aut agrōs [for] nōmen meum [shall receive an hundredfold, and shall inherit] vītam aeternam. (Matthew 19:29)

   [And every one that hath forsaken houses, or] brothers or sisters or father or mother

   or wife or sons or fields [for] my name [shall receive an hundredfold, and shall inherit]

   eternal life.

2. [I call to remembrance the unfeigned faith that is in thee, which dwelt first] in aviā tuā Loide et mātre tuā Eunice. (II Timothy 1:5)

   [I call to remembrance the unfeigned faith that is in thee, which dwelt first]

   in your/thy grandmother Lois and your/thy mother Eunice.

3. [For whosoever shall do the will] Patris meī [which is in heaven, the same] meus frāter et soror et māter est. (Matthew 12:50)

   [For whosoever shall do the will] of my Father [which is in heaven, the same]

   is my brother, and sister, and mother.

4. [But a certain] vir [named] Ananias cum Saffirā uxōre suā [sold a] agrum [and kept back part of the price] agrī, uxor sua [also being privy to it]. (Acts 5:1-2)

   [But a certain] man [named] Ananias with Sapphira his wife [sold a] field

   [and kept back part of the price] of the field, his wife [also being privy to it].

5. [Honor] patrem tuum et matrem. (Ephesians 6:2)

   [Honor] your/thy father and mother.

© 1999 BJU Press. Reproduction prohibited.

Activity P

Match each translation in column 2 with the corresponding Latin phrase in column 1. The italicized words and phrases are added to clarify the literal translations. (In modern use *ad sum* has become one word: *adsum.*)

_I_ 1. ad rem	A.	I am present / I am here
_G_ 2. ars longa, vita brevis	B.	our light *is* from God
_B_ 3. a Deo lux nostra	C.	from God and the king
_E_ 4. a die	D.	from the beginning
_D_ 5. ab initio	E.	from *that* day
_C_ 6. a Deo et rege	F.	to the word / *word for word*
_H_ 7. ad multos annos	G.	art *is* long, life *is* short
_J_ 8. ad patres	H.	for many years
_A_ 9. adsum	I.	to the matter *at hand / to the point*
_F_ 10. ad verbum	J.	*he has gone* to *his* fathers / *he is dead*

Activity Q

In each blank, write the letter for the meaning of the phrase.

_E_ 1. Agnus Dei	A.	before death
_C_ 2. antebellum	B.	after death
_I_ 3. ante cibum	C.	before the war / before the American Civil War
_G_ 4. ante lucem	D.	after the war / after the American Civil War
_A_ 5. ante mortem	E.	the Lamb of God / Christ
_F_ 6. ante omnia	F.	before all things / in the first place
_H_ 7. aut mors aut victoria	G.	before light / before daybreak
_D_ 8. postbellum	H.	either death or victory
_B_ 9. postmortem	I.	before food / (medicine to be taken) before a meal

© 1999 BJU Press. Reproduction prohibited.

This activity reviews the verbs you have been asked to learn in Chapters 1-13. In the blank, write the meaning. Some verbs have more than one meaning, but you are asked to write only one. Since all the verbs except *sum* end in *-t,* your answers should end in *-s:* for example, *walks.* Do not look for the meanings until you have completed the three sections of the activity. Then in the Vocābulārium, find the meanings of any you have forgotten or are not sure of and take time now to learn those meanings. Most verbs in the Vocābulārium have the ending *-ō* instead of *-at, -et,* or *-it.* This ending will be explained in a later chapter.

Part A

1. ambulat _____ *walks (7)*
2. cadit _____ *falls (13)*
3. capit _____ *catches (2)*
4. condit _____ *builds (11)*
5. cūrat _____ *cares for (11)*
6. currit _____ *runs (7)*
7. dat _____ *gives (6)*
8. dēfendit _____ *defends (2)*
9. dīcit _____ *says (2)*
10. dīligit _____ *loves (2)*

Part B

1. discit _____ *learns (2)*
2. docet _____ *teaches (2)*
3. habet _____ *has (2)*
4. iacet (jacet) _____ *lies (7)*
5. intendit _____ *intends (11)*
6. invenit _____ *finds (2)*
7. natat _____ *swims (7)*
8. necat _____ *kills (11)*
9. ostendit _____ *shows (4)*
10. pascit _____ *feeds (2)*

Part C

1. praebet _____ *offers (6)*
2. pugnat _____ *fights (12)*
3. sedet _____ *sits (7)*
4. servat _____ *saves (11)*
5. stat _____ *stands (7)*
6. sum _____ *I am (5)*
7. est _____ *is (1)*
8. timet _____ *fears (2)*

© 1999 BJU Press. Reproduction prohibited.

CAPITULUM XIV

Give brief Latin answers to these questions, basing your answers on the Latin paragraph entitled "Wars." Put each noun and adjective in the case it would be if your answer were a complete sentence.

1. Who was a Roman general? _____ *Iūlius/Julius Caesar* _____

2. What kind of army did he have? _____ *fortem* _____

3. What did Caesar's army do? _____ *Magnam partem Eurōpae vincēbat / Vincēbat magnam....* _____

4. What do many countries in Europe still do? _____ *Pugnant / Pugnant bella.* _____

5. What wars do books of history tell about? _____ *dē antīquīs et recentibus bellīs* _____

6. Will there be future wars? _____ *Erunt / Ita vērē erunt.* _____

Activity B

Give one of the possible translations for each verb. Then for numbers 1-4, change the Latin verb to the imperfect tense, plural number, and translate the verb that you write. For numbers 5-8, change the imperfect tense, plural number to the present tense, singular number, and translate the verb that you write. **English translations will vary.**

1. clāmat _____ *(1) he shouts / (2) clāmābant / (3) they were shouting* _____

2. ambulat _____ *(1) he walks / (2) ambulābant / (3) they were walking* _____

3. necat _____ *(1) he kills / (2) necābant / (3) they were killing* _____

4. servat _____ *(1) he saves / (2) servābant / (3) they were saving* _____

5. natābant _____ *(1) they were swimming / (2) natat / (3) he swims* _____

6. cūrābant _____ *(1) they were caring for / (2) cūrat / (3) he is caring for* _____

7. pugnābant _____ *(1) they were fighting / (2) pugnat / (3) he fights* _____

8. interrogābant _____ *(1) they were asking / (2) interrogat / (3) he asks* _____

© 1999 BJU Press. Reproduction prohibited.

Translate each sentence. In sentences 1-5, translate into English; in sentences 6-8, translate into Latin. **Accept other possible verb translations as shown on page 191.**

1. Magister magnum librum habet. _____

   _____ *The teacher has a large book.* _____

2. Discipulīs partem° librī legēbat. _____

   _____ *He/She was reading / read part of the book to the pupils.* _____

   [°part]

3. Liber vītam Caesaris narrat. _____

   _____ *The book narrates/tells the life of Caesar.* _____

4. Exercitus Caesaris patriās aliās° pugnābat. _____

   _____ *Caesar's army was fighting / fought other countries.* _____

   [°other]

5. Discipulī dē bellīs° Caesaris discēbant. _____

   _____ *The pupils were learning / learned about the wars of Caesar / Caesar's wars.* _____

   [°war]

6. The pupils have a good teacher. _____

   _____ *Discipulī magistrum bonum / magistram bonam habent.* _____

7. The teacher was teaching about Rome. _____

   _____ *Magister/Magistra dē Rōmā docēbat.* _____

8. The pupils were learning well. _____

   _____ *Discipulī bene discēbant.* _____

© 1999 BJU Press. Reproduction prohibited.

Complete these translations of portions of Latin verses from the Gospel of Mark by filling in the blanks. **Verb translations will vary. Accept uppercase or lowercase for *He, Him,* and *His.* They are not capitalized in the Greek.**

1. Cōnveniēbant° ad eum undique°. (1:45)

   They were coming together to him from all sides.

   [°come together; °from all sides]

2. Omnis turba° veniēbat° ad eum et docēbat eōs. (2:13)

   All the crowd was coming / came to him and he was teaching them.

   [°crowd; °come]

3. Scrībae et Pharisaeī dīcēbant discipulīs eius. (2:16)

   The scribes and the Pharisees were speaking/talking to his disciples.

4. Pharisaeī autem° dīcēbant eī. (2:24)

   The Pharisees moreover were speaking/saying/talking to him.

   [°moreover]

5. Et dīcēbat eīs. (2:27)

   And he was speaking/saying/talking to them.

6. Consilium° faciēbant° adversus eum. (3:6)

   They were making a plan against him.

   [°plan; °make]

7. Et spiritūs inmundī° clāmābant°, dīcentēs° tū es Fīlius Deī. (3:11)

   And unclean spirits were shouting, saying you are the Son of God.

   [°unclean spirits; °shout, cry out; °saying]

8. Et docēbat eōs in parabolīs. (4:2)

   And he was teaching them in parables.

9. Et inrīdēbant° eum. (5:40)

   And they were ridiculing him.

   [°ridicule, laugh at]

10. Interrogābant° eum discipulī eius parabolam°. (7:17)

    The disciples were asking him about his parable.

    [°ask; °about his parable]

© 1999 BJU Press. Reproduction prohibited.

In the first two blanks for each verb, write the translation of the principal parts; in the third blank, write *1st, 2nd, 3rd,* or *4th* to show which conjugation the verb is.

1. ambulō, ambulāre ___I walk___ ___to walk___ ___1st___

2. capiō, capere ___I take___ ___to take___ ___3rd___

3. iaceō, iacēre ___I lie/rest___ ___to lie/rest___ ___2nd___

4. dīcō, dīcere ___I say___ ___to say___ ___3rd___

5. habeō, habēre ___I have___ ___to have___ ___2nd___

6. pugnō, pugnāre ___I fight___ ___to fight___ ___1st___

7. timeō, timēre ___I fear___ ___to fear___ ___2nd___

8. veniō, venīre [come] ___I come___ ___to come___ ___4th___

Without looking at the chapter, write in the first column *1st, 2nd, 3rd,* or *4th* to name the conjugation of each infinitive.

For verbs in the second column write (1) the Latin pronoun subject and (2) the translation of the verb (without any auxiliary), including its pronoun subject. (Use the masculine form for third-person pronouns.) Then check your work, using the information in the chapter.

1. stare ___1st___ stas ___tū___ ___you stand___

2. iacēre ___2nd___ iacent ___eī___ ___they lie/rest___

3. ambulāre ___1st___ ambulāmus ___nōs___ ___we walk___

4. dīcere ___3rd___ dīcētis ___vōs___ ___you say___

5. pascere ___3rd___ pascit ___is___ ___he feeds___

6. praebēre ___2nd___ praebent ___eī___ ___they offer___

7. ostendere ___3rd___ ostendō ___ego___ ___I show___

8. natāre ___1st___ natās ___tū___ ___you (sing.) swim___

9. invenīre ___4th___ invenītis ___vōs___ ___you (pl.) find___

© 1999 BJU Press. Reproduction prohibited.

Match the translations in column 2 with the Latin verbs in column 1. (One letter will not be used.) If you must look in the Vocābulārium for help, take time right now to learn the meaning of each word you look up.

_A_	1. stābant	A.	they were standing
_H_	2. praebent	B.	they were biting
_B_	3. mordēbant	C.	you (sing.) find
_E_	4. celebrāmus	D.	you (pl.) did have
_F_	5. dēfendō	E.	we are celebrating
_G_	6. natābāmus	F.	I defend
_K_	7. servābāmus	G.	we were swimming
_D_	8. habēbātis	H.	they offer (provide)
_J_	9. scrībō	I.	we will go
_C_	10. invenīs	J.	I am writing
		K.	we were keeping (saving)

Activity H

Write each of the following brief sentences in Latin. Put correct case endings on the Latin nouns as well as the correct inflections on the verbs.

1. Brave men were fighting the Romans. _____

   Virī fortēs Rōmānōs pugnābant.

2. Were they celebrating the great victory? _____

   Celebrābantne magnam victōriam?

3. History tells about the great victory. _____

   Historia dē magnā victōriā / victōriā magnā narrat.

4. The teacher was telling the pupils about life in Rome. _____

   Magister/Magistra discipulīs dē vītā in Rōmā narrābat.

5. Are you asking about the history of Greece? _____

   Interrogātisne/Interrogāsne dē historiā Graeciae?

© 1999 BJU Press. Reproduction prohibited.

Translate the sentences. Most of them are not complete verses because the rest of the verse contains grammar you have not yet studied.

1. Advocātum° apud° Patrem habēmus, Jēsum Christum. (I John 2:1)

   We have an advocate before the Father, Jesus Christ.

   [°advocate; °before, in the presence of]

2. Nōs ex Deō sumus. (I John 4:6)

   We are from God.

3. Pācem habēmus apud° Deum, per Dominum nostrum Jēsum Christum. (Romans 5:1)

   We have peace with God through our Lord Jesus Christ.

   [°with, in the presence of]

4. Ecce°, veniō° citō°. (Revelation 22:12)

   Behold, I come quickly.

   [°behold; °come; °quickly, suddenly]

5. Ecce, leprosus° adorābat° eum°. (Matthew 8:2)

   Behold, a leper was worshiping/adoring him.

   [°leper; °worship; °him]

6. Petrus dē naviculā° ambulābat super° aquam. (Matthew 14:29)

   Peter was walking from the boat upon the water.

   [°little ship (boat); °upon]

7. [The disciples said,] vērē Fīlius Deī es. (Matthew 14:33)

   [The disciples said,] Truly, you are the Son of God. / Truly thou art the Son of God.

8. [The centurions and the guards said,] vērē Deī Fīlius erat. (Matthew 27:54)

   [The centurions and the guards said,] Truly He was the Son of God.

© 1999 BJU Press. Reproduction prohibited.

Write each sentence in English. Then change the Latin verb to the imperfect tense and translate just that one word.

1. Senātus est magnus.

The senate is large.	erat	was

2. Nōs sumus senātōrēs.

We are senators.	erāmus	We were

3. Esne quoque° senātor?

Are you also a senator?	Erāsne	Were you

   [°also]

4. Ita vērē, sum senātor.

Yes truly, I am a senator.	eram	I was

5. Senātōrēs sunt amīcī meī.

The senators are my friends.	erant	were

6. Esne tū novus° in senātū?

Are you new in the senate?	erāsne	Were you

   [°new]

Write each sentence in Latin. Use pronoun subjects in some of the sentences.

1. In Christ we are free. *In Christō (nōs) sumus līberī.*

2. We have peace through Christ. *(Nōs) pācem per Christum habēmus.*

3. We are Christians. *(Nōs) sumus Christiānī.*

4. You (pl.) are sheep of the Shepherd. *(Vōs) estis agnī Pastōris.*

5. [Jesus said,] Ye are my friends. *(Vōs) estis amīcī meī.*

© 1999 BJU Press. Reproduction prohibited.

Activity L

For each phrase, write the letter for the phrase that explains the underlined derivative.

_G_ 1. an <u>ambulatory</u> patient   A. inclined to fight

_H_ 2. an <u>exclamation</u>   B. the act of keeping or saving

_D_ 3. an <u>interrogation</u>   C. an indoor swimming pool

_A_ 4. a <u>pugnacious</u> man   D. a questioning

_F_ 5. a firm <u>stance</u>   E. a story

_E_ 6. a <u>narration</u>   F. standing position

_C_ 7. a <u>natatorium</u>   G. able to walk

_B_ 8. <u>preservation</u> of resources   H. a calling out; an abrupt, forceful statement

Activity M

This review can help you remember the infinitives of several verbs you have worked with in this chapter. Write the English meaning of the infinitive of each verb: for example, "to stand." (That is the form that is used in definitions in the Vocābulārium and in Latin dictionaries.) Then say aloud the two forms of each verb, being careful to place the accent correctly. Remember that when the penult is short, the accent is on the antepenult.

When you have written the meanings of all the verbs you can recall, check your answers with the lists in the chapter. For any that you missed or left blank, take time *now* to memorize the two verb forms and the dictionary meaning.

1. doceō, docēre _to teach_

2. dīcō, dīcere _to say/speak_

3. narrō, narrāre _to tell_

4. audiō, audīre _to hear_

5. ambulō, ambulāre _to walk_

6. capiō, capere _to take_

7. iaceō, iacēre _to lie/rest_

8. habeō, habēre _to have_

9. pugnō, pugnāre _to fight_

10. timeō, timēre _to fear_

11. veniō, venīre _to come_

12. sum, esse _to be_

© 1999 BJU Press. Reproduction prohibited.

CAPITULUM XV

In the Latin paragraphs about Roman religion, find each noun listed below and give its case and number. Note carefully how each noun is used in the sentence. You may abbreviate.

1. Rōmānōrum _____*gen. pl.*_____

2. religiōnī _____*dat. sing.*_____

3. deās _____*acc. pl.*_____

4. Neptūnus _____*nom. sing.*_____

5. Plūto _____*nom. sing.*_____

6. Christiānī _____*nom. pl.*_____

7. Deum _____*acc. sing.*_____

Find each verb in the paragraphs and give its tense and number. In Chapter 14 you saw that regular verbs with the tense sign *bā* are in the imperfect tense, but the *be* verb is irregular.

8. erat _____*imperf. sing.*_____

9. habēbant _____*imperf. pl.*_____

10. timēbant _____*imperf. pl.*_____

11. erant _____*imperf. pl.*_____

12. adōrant _____*pres. pl.*_____

Circle the number that shows the person of all five verbs listed above: *first, second,* *third.*

© 1999 BJU Press. Reproduction prohibited.

Answer each question briefly. Use case and number forms that you would use in a complete sentence.

1. Religiō quōrum° erat similis religiōnī Rōmānōrum? _____ *Religiō Graecōrum / Graecōrum*
   [°whose, of whom]

2. Timēbantne Graecī deōs? _____ *Ita vērē timēbant / Deōs timēbant.*

3. Eratne Neptūnus deus maior aut minor? _____ *maior*

4. Erantne Vesta et Cerēs deī aut deae? _____ *deae*

5. Quem Christiānī adōrant? _____ *Deum ūnum vērum*

Activity C

Write the present tense form of each verb according to the description given. Translate each verb, using any one of the three possible English translations. However, use each of the three possible English translations at least once. **Translations will vary. Each possible translation should be used at least once.**

1. natō, -āre—third person plural _____ *natant—they swim*

2. timeō, -ēre—second person plural _____ *timētis—you are fearing*

3. iaceō, -ēre—first person plural _____ *iacēmus—we are lying/resting*

4. veniō, -īre—third person plural _____ *veniunt—they do come*

5. pascō, -ere—second person singular _____ *pascis—you feed*

6. audiō, -īre—second person singular _____ *audīs—you do hear*

7. intendō, -ere—third person plural _____ *intendunt—they plan*

8. legō, -ere—third person singular _____ *legit—he is reading*

9. doceō, -ēre—first person plural _____ *docēmus—we teach*

10. vocō, -āre—third person singular _____ *vocat—he is calling*

© 1999 BJU Press. Reproduction prohibited.

© 1999 BJU Press. Reproduction prohibited.

Activity D

Write each sentence in Latin, paying particular attention to the vowels that precede the inflections. If you have forgotten the word for *children,* return to the list of family members in Chapter 13. **Verb forms will vary.**

1. You (sing.) are teaching. _____ *Docēs.* _____

2. We hear our teacher. _____ *Magistrum nostrum / Magistram nostram audīmus.* _____

3. Are the children learning the Latin language? _____ *Discuntne līberī linguam Latīnam?* _____
   _____

4. I take my book. _____ *Librum meum capiō.* _____

5. Are you (pl.) taking the books? _____ *Capitisne librōs?* _____

Activity E

Write the imperfect tense of each verb according to the description given. For numbers 1-5, write the translation that clearly shows continued action in the past. **Accept either long or short *a* in *stabant.***

1. stō, stare—third person plural _____ *stābant—they were standing* _____

2. scrībō, -ere—second person plural _____ *scrībēbātis—you were writing* _____

3. inveniō, -īre—third person singular _____ *inveniēbat—he was finding* _____

4. sedeō, -ēre—second person singular _____ *sedēbās—you were sitting* _____

5. superō, -āre—first person plural _____ *superābāmus—we were overcoming* _____

6. cadō, -ere—first person plural _____ *cadēbāmus* _____

7. faciō, -ere—first person singular _____ *faciēbam* _____

8. capiō, -ere—third person singular _____ *capiēbat* _____

9. trānsiliō, -ere—third person plural _____ *trānsiliēbant* _____

10. currō, -ere—first person singular _____ *currēbam* _____

Activity F

Write these sentences in Latin. If necessary, use the Vocābulārium or the list of family names in Chapter 13. Remember that pronoun subjects are often omitted in Latin sentences.

1. I was writing a book. _____
   _____ *Librum scrībēbam. / Ego librum scrībēbam.* _____

2. My sister was reading a good book. _____
   _____ *Soror mea librum bonum legēbat.* _____

3. The women were speaking. _____
   _____ *Mulierēs/Fēminae dīcēbant.* _____

4. Were you (sing.) hearing the oration? _____
   _____ *Audiēbāsne ōrātiōnem? / Audiēbāsne tū ōrātiōnem?* _____

5. We did not fear the leader. _____
   _____ *Ducem nōn timēbāmus. / Nōs ducem nōn timēbāmus.* _____

6. Are you (pl.) doing the work? _____
   _____ *Facitisne opus? / Vōs facitisne opus?* _____

7. They told us many legends. _____
   _____ *Nōbīs multās fabulās narrābant.* _____

Activity G

Write these sentences in Latin. Be accurate in the use of stem vowels, tense signs, and personal inflections.

1. The disciples were walking with the Lord to the city. _____
   _____ *Discipulī cum Dominō ad urbem ambulābant.* _____

2. Jesus was teaching the disciples. _____
   _____ *Iēsus discipulōs docēbat.* _____

3. The disciples heard the words of Christ. _____
   _____ *Discipulī verba Christī audiēbant.* _____

4. Do you (pl.) read the words of Scripture? _____
   _____ *Legitisne verba Scriptūrae?* _____

© 1999 BJU Press. Reproduction prohibited.

Activity H

Give brief Latin answers. Use noun and adjective cases that you would use in sentence answers. In number 4, one genitive-case noun modifies another genitive-case noun.

1. Quī° deōs pāgānōs faciēbant? _____ *mortālēs/virī* _____
   [°who]

2. Audiuntne deī pāgānī ubi° pāgānī supplicant? _____ *Nōn audiunt.* _____
   [°when]

3. Quālis Deus nōbīs vēritātem ostendit? _____ *vērus / vērus Deus / ūnus vērus Deus* _____

4. Quī adōrant opus manuum virōrum? _____ *mortālēs / virī / virī pāgānī* _____

Activity I

In the blanks write (1) the preposition, (2) the root form of the verb (the infinitive form), and (3) the literal meaning, putting the root word before the prefix in the meaning. Omit the meaning of the prefix if it intensifies the root word.

Example: invoke _____*in*_____ _____*vocāre*_____ _____*to call in*_____

1. perambulate _____*per*_____ _____*ambulāre*_____ _____*to walk through*_____

2. concur _____*cum*_____ _____*currere*_____ _____*to run with/together*_____

3. conserve _____*cum*_____ _____*servāre*_____ _____*to save*_____

4. convene _____*cum*_____ _____*venīre*_____ _____*to come together*_____

5. convince _____*cum*_____ _____*vincere*_____ _____*to conquer*_____

6. inscribe _____*in*_____ _____*scrībere*_____ _____*to write on*_____

7. deduce _____*dē*_____ _____*ducere*_____ _____*to lead down from*_____

Activity J

Write each italicized word or phrase in Latin. Although some of these pronouns are not needed in a Latin sentence, write them in order to emphasize the subject.

1. He gave *me* a ticket to the game. _____ *mihi* _____

2. Will you go *with me* to the game? _____ *cum mē / mēcum* _____

3. I am inviting *you* (sing.) to the picnic. _____ *tē* _____

4. *I* hope you will come. _____ *Ego* _____

5. *You* (sing.) may bring a friend *with you.* _____ *Tū cum tē / tēcum* _____

6. Please give *us* your reply by Friday. _____ *nōbīs* _____

7. *We* really want you to come. _____ *Nōs* _____

8. A few *of us* have never been to Buena Vista Park before. _____ *nostrum* _____

© 1999 BJU Press. Reproduction prohibited.

In this activity you have portions of verses from the Gospel of John. Translate the Latin portion of the verses without referring to your Bible. Each verse contains (1) a personal pronoun or (2) an adjective that shows possession. Pay close attention to the case of each pronoun and adjective. This activity does not contain examples of genitive of the whole or objective genitive. (Verse references are from the Vulgate.)

1. [The priests and Levites asked John the Baptist,] quis tū es? (1:19)

   ___who are you?___

2. [John the Baptist confessed,] nōn sum ego Christus. (1:20)

   ___I am not (the) Christ.___

3. [Then they asked him, why do you baptize if] tū nōn es Christus? (1:25)

   ___you are not (the) Christ?___

4. [John said, one stands in the midst of you whom] vōs nōn scītis°. (1:26)

   ___you do not know.___

   [°know]

5. [Nathaniel said, Rabbi,] tū es Fīlius Deī, tū es Rēx Israel. (1:49)

   ___you are the Son of God, you are the King of Israel.___

6. [Jesus said, truly, truly,] dīcō vōbīs. . . . (1:51)

   ___I say to you (pl.)___

7. [Jesus said to Nicodemus,] dīcō tibi. . . . (3:3)

   ___I say to you (sing.)___

8. Et nōs ___And we___ [have believed and know that] tū es Christus, Fīlius

   Deī. (6:70) ___you are / thou art Christ, the Son of God.___

9. [Philip said, Lord show] nōbīs Patrem. (14:8) ___to us / us the Father.___

10. [The woman at the well said,] patrēs nostrī ___our fathers___

    [worshipped on this mountain]. (4:20)

11. [Jesus said,] meus cibus° est ___my food is___ [to do the will of him

    which sent me]. (4:34)

    [°food]

12. [Jesus said to Martha,] frāter tuus ___your brother___ [will rise again].

    (11:23)

© 1999 BJU Press. Reproduction prohibited.

Write the first two principal parts of these verbs without referring to the list in this chapter or to the Vocābulārium. Then check your answers for accuracy and circle the numbers of any that you omitted or wrote incorrectly. Take time to learn those verbs.

1. to jump across ___*trānsiliō, -īre*___
2. to jump into ___*insiliō, -īre*___
3. to swim ___*natō, -āre*___
4. to run ___*currō, -ere*___
5. to walk ___*ambulō, -āre*___
6. to stand ___*stō, -are*___
7. to sit ___*sedeō, -ēre*___
8. to lie (rest) ___*iaceō, -ēre*___
9. to teach ___*doceō, -ēre*___
10. to learn ___*discō, -ere*___
11. to hear ___*audiō, -īre*___
12. to read ___*legō, -ere*___
13. to write ___*scrībō, -ere*___
14. to speak ___*dīcō, -ere*___

15. to sing ___*cantō, -āre*___
16. to call ___*vocō, -āre*___
17. to tell a story ___*narrō, -āre*___
18. to come ___*veniō, -īre*___
19. to find ___*inveniō, -īre*___
20. to fear ___*timeō, -ēre*___
21. to live ___*vīvō, -ere*___
22. to fight ___*pugnō, -āre*___
23. to conquer ___*superō, -āre / vincō, -ere*___
24. to increase ___*crescō, -ere*___
25. to plan ___*intendō, -ere*___
26. to build ___*condō, -ere / construō, -ere*___
27. to show ___*ostendō, -ere*___

© 1999 BJU Press. Reproduction prohibited.

CAPITULUM XVI

Write *Vērum* or *Falsum* before each statement. The content of the sentences is based on Magister's explanation of events in the early Roman republic and on the Latin paragraph entitled "Anserēs." If any statement is not mentioned in Magister's discussion, consider the sentence to be false.

The meanings of some new words are not given because their contexts and their similarity to English derivatives make the meanings obvious.

__*Vērum*__ 1. Gallī ad Etruscōs in paeninsulā Ītaliā erant.

(The Gauls were near the Etruscans in/on the Italian peninsula.)

__*Vērum*__ 2. Gallī terram ab Etruscīs capiēbant.

(The Gauls captured land from the Etruscans.)

__*Falsum*__ 3. Ūnus° mīles Rōmānus erat amīcus mīlitibus Gallicīs.

[°one] **(One Roman soldier was friendly to the Gallic soldiers.)**

__*Vērum*__ 4. Anserēs erant sacrī° deae.

[°sacred] **(Geese were sacred to a goddess.)**

__*Falsum*__ 5. Mīlitēs Gallicī in arce erant.

(The Gallic soldiers were in the citadel.)

__*Vērum*__ 6. Mīlitēs Rōmānī ab mīlitibus Gallīs currēbant.

(The Roman soldiers ran from the Gallic soldiers.)

__*Falsum*__ 7. Anserēs vītās mīlitum Gallōrum servābant.

(The geese saved the lives of the Gallic soldiers.)

© 1999 BJU Press. Reproduction prohibited.

Activity B

From what you learn in the paragraph, give short Latin answers to these questions. Be sure that the forms are what they would be in complete sentences. Try not to go through the translation process to arrive at your answers. **Answers will vary.**

1. Quī contrā Gallōs pugnābant? _____ *Rōmānī*

2. Cur Gallī exsultābant? _____ *propter victōriam in proeliō contrā Rōmānōs*

3. Quī ex proeliō currēbant? _____ *Rōmānī / mīlitēs Rōmānī*

4. Ubi familiae Rōmānae fugiēbant? _____ *ex urbe ad locum tutum*

5. Ubi mīlitēs Rōmānī ascendēbant? _____ *in arcem*

6. Quī quoque° ad arcem veniēbant? _____ *Gallī / mīlitēs Gallī*
   [°also]

7. Ubī anserēs strīdōrem faciēbant? _____ *noctū*

8. Quid agunt° Rōmānī ubi anserēs audiēbant? _____ *Gallōs repellēbant.*
   [°do]

Activity C

Write these verbs in the future tense. To get them right, you must know the infinitives. Refer to the verb list in Chapter 15 if necessary. Strive for absolute accuracy.

1. we will swim _____ *natābimus*

2. we will take _____ *capiēmus*

3. you (sing.) will teach _____ *docēbis*

4. we will run _____ *currēmus*

5. they will fight _____ *pugnābunt*

6. they will take _____ *capient*

7. they will be _____ *erunt*

8. you (pl.) will call _____ *vocābitis*

9. we will write _____ *scrībēmus*

10. you (sing.) will be _____ *eris*

11. I will fear _____ *timēbō*

12. I will come _____ *veniam*

13. he will have _____ *habēbit*

14. I will take _____ *capiam*

15. we will hear _____ *audiēmus*

© 1999 BJU Press. Reproduction prohibited.

Translate each sentence. The tense may be present, imperfect, or future. Remember that verbs other than forms of the *be* verb are ***usually*** at the end of the sentence. Variations of word order are frequent, as you will note in numbers 5, 6, and 9.

1. Ad lacum ambulābit. _____
   _____
   He/She will walk to the lake.

2. Montem ascendiam. _____
   _____
   I will ascend / climb up the/a mountain.

3. Quercūs post mūrem stant. _____
   _____
   Oak trees stand / are standing behind the wall.

4. Agnus in terrā iacēbat. _____
   _____
   A lamb was lying on the ground.

5. Veniētisne ad Rōmam? _____
   _____
   Will you come to Rome?

6. Legēsne librum meum dē historiā Rōmae? _____
   _____
   Will you read my book about the history of Rome?

7. Senātor dīcēbat, "Caesar mīlitēs dūcet." _____
   _____
   A/The senator said / did say / was saying, "Caesar will lead the soldiers."

8. Caesar Gallōs vincēbat. _____
   _____
   Caesar conquered / was conquering the Gauls.

9. Legam dē bellīs ubi Caesar erat dux. _____
   _____
   I will read about the wars when Caesar was a/the leader/general.

10. Ubi Caesar erat dux, Rōma erat rēs° publica°. _____
    _____
    When Caesar was a general, Rome was a republic.

[°republic (Two words became one.)]

© 1999 BJU Press. Reproduction prohibited.

Activity E

Translate each Latin word. (1) Determine the conjugation of each regular verb from its infinitive. (2) For the *first* present tense verb listed and the *first* imperfect tense verb listed, give all the possible translations. (3) For the others, give one of the possible translations. (4) For the future tense verbs, use the auxiliary *will*. If necessary, refer to the Vocābulārium. Strive for perfection. **Auxiliaries in answers will vary.**

1. cantāmus — *we sing / we are singing / we do sing*

2. cantābāmus — *we sang / we were singing / we did sing*

3. cantābimus — *we will sing*

4. praebēbunt — *they will offer*

5. praebēmus — *we offer*

6. veniētis — *you (pl.) will come*

7. dīcēbāmus — *we said*

8. stābis — *you (sing.) will stand*

9. erō — *I will be*

10. erātis — *you (pl.) were*

11. es — *you are*

12. fugient — *they will flee*

13. inveniam — *I will find*

14. pascēbant — *they were feeding*

15. ascendis — *you climb*

© 1999 BJU Press. Reproduction prohibited.

© 1999 BJU Press. Reproduction prohibited.

Activity F

Translate each sentence, giving special attention to the tense of the verbs.

1. Lupus nōn mordet lupum. (Medieval Latin saying) _____
   A wolf does not bite a wolf.

2. Rotam° Fortūnae° nōn timent. (Cicero) _____
   They do not fear the wheel of Fortune.
   [°wheel; °Fortune, Roman goddess of luck or chance]

3. Crēscetne pecūnia ab manū Fortūnae? _____
   Will money increase from the hand of Fortune?

4. Magistrī puerīs parvīs crustula° dant. (Horace) _____
   Teachers give small boys cookies.
   [°cookies]

5. Dīligentne puerī parvī magistrum propter crustula? _____
   Will small boys love the teacher on account of the cookies?

6. Semper° glōria et fāma tua manēbunt°. (Virgil) _____
   Your glory and fame will always remain.
   [°always; °remain]

7. Propter cūram° meam in perpetuō° perīculō° nōn eritis. (Cicero) _____
   Because of my care you will not be in constant danger.
   [°care; °perpetual, constant; °danger]

Activity G

Determine the noun function of each infinitive: subject or direct object. In each blank, write *S* or *DO*.

_____**S**_____ 1. Errāre est hūmānum. (Seneca, a Stoic philosopher) ("To err is human.")
   (Errāre means "to wander from the right path, to make a mistake.")

_____**DO**_____ 2. Bonī propter amōrem virtūtis peccāre ōdērunt. (Horace, a Roman poet) ("Good people on account of love of virtue hate to sin.")
   (Bonī modifies the understood subject people.)

_____**S**_____ 3. Mutāre nātūram est difficile. (Anonymous) ("To change nature is difficult.")

_____**DO**_____ 4. Audeō dīcere. (Julius Caesar) ("I dare to speak.")

_____**S**_____ 5. Rēs est magna tacēre. (Anonymous) ("To be silent is a great thing.")
   ("It is a great thing to be silent." It is an expletive. Latin does not have a parallel use of it.)

Activity H

Translate the Latin portions of these sentences; in the second blank, write the Latin verb that is completed by the infinitive.

1. [He that says that he lives in Christ] dēbet ambulāre [even as He walked].

   (I John 2:6) _____*he ought to walk*_____ _____*dēbet*_____

2. [Beloved, if God so loved us,] nōs dēbēmus dīligere [one another].

   (I John 4:11) _____*we ought to love*_____ _____*dēbēmus*_____

3. [Receive with meekness the engrafted word, which] potest servāre animās° vestrās.

   (James 1:21) _____*is able to save your souls*_____ _____*potest*_____
   [°soul]

4. [Thomas asked the Lord, how] possumus viam scīre? (John 14:5)

   _____*are we able to know the way?*_____ _____*possumus*_____

Activity I

Read each sentence carefully. Find the infinitive and decide whether it is used as a noun or a complementary infinitive. Then write in the blank *Noun* or *Comp.* and translate each sentence.

___*Noun*___ 1. Pugnāre contrā Gallōs erat voluntās Caesaris.

To fight against the Gauls was the will/wish of Caesar.

___

___*Comp.*___ 2. Prīmō Rōmānōs Gallī vincere poterant°.

At first the Gauls were able to overcome the Romans.

___

___*Noun*___ 3. Tum nocte° Gallī ad castra° Rōmāna veniēbant. Anserēs strīdōrem facere incipiēbant°.

Then at night the Gauls were coming near the Roman camp.

The geese began to make a loud noise.

[°at night; °camp; °begin]

___*Comp.*___ 4. Mīlitēs Rōmānī Gallōs repellere poterant.

The Roman soldiers were able to drive back the Gauls.

___

© 1999 BJU Press. Reproduction prohibited.

Write each sentence in Latin. Write the pronoun subjects in sentences that do not have noun subjects.

1. I gave a horse to him. ⎯⎯⎯⎯⎯⎯⎯⎯⎯⎯⎯⎯⎯⎯⎯⎯
   ⎯⎯⎯⎯⎯⎯⎯⎯*Ego equum eī dābam.*⎯⎯⎯⎯⎯⎯⎯⎯⎯⎯⎯⎯⎯

2. His farm is small. ⎯⎯⎯⎯⎯⎯⎯⎯⎯⎯⎯⎯⎯⎯⎯⎯⎯⎯
   ⎯⎯⎯⎯⎯⎯⎯⎯⎯*Ager eius est parvus.*⎯⎯⎯⎯⎯⎯⎯⎯⎯⎯⎯⎯⎯

3. He and Quintus give food° to their horses. ⎯⎯⎯⎯⎯⎯⎯⎯⎯⎯
   ⎯⎯⎯⎯⎯⎯*Is et Quintus equīs eōrum cibum dant.*⎯⎯⎯⎯⎯⎯⎯⎯⎯
   [°cibum]

4. They lead their horses to water. ⎯⎯⎯⎯⎯⎯⎯⎯⎯⎯⎯⎯⎯
   ⎯⎯⎯⎯⎯⎯*Eī equōs eōrum ad aquam dūcunt.*⎯⎯⎯⎯⎯⎯⎯⎯⎯

5. They build their horses a barn°. ⎯⎯⎯⎯⎯⎯⎯⎯⎯⎯⎯⎯⎯
   ⎯⎯⎯⎯⎯⎯*Eī equīs eōrum horreum condunt.*⎯⎯⎯⎯⎯⎯⎯⎯⎯
   [°horreum]

6. It is large. ⎯⎯⎯⎯⎯⎯⎯⎯⎯⎯⎯⎯⎯⎯⎯⎯⎯⎯⎯⎯⎯
   ⎯⎯⎯⎯⎯⎯⎯⎯⎯⎯*Id est magnum.*⎯⎯⎯⎯⎯⎯⎯⎯⎯⎯⎯⎯

7. Their sisters, Cornelia and Fulvia, also have horses. ⎯⎯⎯⎯⎯⎯⎯
   ⎯⎯⎯*Sorōrēs eōrum, Cornēlia et Fulvia, quoque equōs habent.*⎯⎯⎯

8. Their [the sisters'] horses run fast°. ⎯⎯⎯⎯⎯⎯⎯⎯⎯⎯⎯⎯⎯
   ⎯⎯⎯⎯⎯⎯⎯*Equī eārum rapidē currunt.*⎯⎯⎯⎯⎯⎯⎯⎯⎯⎯
   [°rapidǫ]

© 1999 BJU Press. Reproduction prohibited.

Translate each of these sentences taken from the Gospel of John. Parts of sentences that you cannot translate at this time are in brackets. Some of the information in brackets is added to give you a clear context of the verse. In your translations, include the bracketed English portions, except for the long introductory portions.

1. Dīcit eī Jēsus, [Go], fīlius tuus vīvit. (4:50)

   Jesus says to him, [Go], your son lives / is living.

2. Jēsus autem respondet eīs, Pater meus [works until now, and I work]. (5:17)

   Moreover/However Jesus responds to them, my Father [works until now, and I work].

3. [Some Jews sought to slay Jesus because He said that God was His Father. Jesus said to them, his Word] nōn habētis [remaining] in vōbīs. (5:38)

   You do not have [his Word remaining] in you.

4. [Jesus said, This is the] voluntās° ejus quī mīsit° mē [that whosoever sees] Fīlium et credit° in eum [may have] vītam aeternam. (6:40)
   [°will, wish; °sent; °believe]

   [Jesus said, This is the] will of him / his will who [sent] me [that whosoever sees]

   the Son and believes upon him [may have] eternal life.

5. Dīcit eīs Nicodemus, is quī [had come] ad eum [at night]. . . . (7:50)

   Nicodemus speaks to them, he who [had come] to him [at night]. . . .

6. [In the temple] populus [came] ad eum, et [sitting down] docēbat eōs. (8:2)

   [In the temple] the people [came] to him, and [sitting down] he taught them.

7. Tum° [Jesus said] eīs, Id quod° [was] ā principiō° dīcō vōbīs. (8:25)

   Then [Jesus said] to them, I speak/say to you that which [was] from the beginning.

   [°then; °which; °beginning]

© 1999 BJU Press. Reproduction prohibited.

For each underlined word, write the Latin word from which the derivative came and the meaning of the Latin word. If two sets of blanks are given, the derivative is a combination of two Latin words.

If the Latin word is a verb, give only the infinitive form. If it is a noun, give only its genitive singular form. You may look at the lists on pages 215 and 227 if necessary.

1. It is impolite to <u>contradict</u> your elders (people older than you).

   __*contrā*__ __*against*__ ; __*dīcere*__ __*to speak*__

2. Owls and bats are <u>nocturnal</u> creatures.

   __*noctū*__ __*at night*__

3. The <u>strident</u> sounds of the flock of cranes awoke me early this morning.

   __*strīdōris*__ __*loud/harsh noise*__

4. The <u>military</u> forces of the United States are under the authority of the president.

   __*militis*__ __*soldier*__

5. The <u>fugitives</u> escaped through a secret tunnel.

   __*fugere*__ __*to flee*__

6. The <u>ascent</u> to the summit of Mount Everest is not for the unprepared.

   __*ascendere*__ __*to climb up*__

7. The group <u>ambled</u> along at a leisurely pace.

   __*ambulāre*__ __*to walk*__

8. The <u>location</u> of the camp was near a lake.

   __*locus*__ __*place*__

9. John was not drafted into the United States Marine Corps; he entered the service as a <u>volunteer</u>.

   __*voluntātis*__ __*will/wish*__

10. Jim gave a <u>credible</u> excuse for his absence.

    __*crēdere*__ __*to believe*__

© 1999 BJU Press. Reproduction prohibited.

This review of Latin words covers the chapters you have studied thus far. You will see several ways that English derivatives have come from Latin words, and you will probably discover some English words you have never seen or heard (especially in numbers 11-12).

Latin word : English derivative :: Latin word : English derivative

1. exultāre : exult :: ascendere : _____ascend_____

2. cūrāre : cure :: scrībere : _____scribe_____

3. narrāre : narration :: vocāre : _____vocation_____

4. celebrāre : celebrate :: suffōcāre : _____suffocate_____

5. sēcrētus : secret :: longus : _____long_____

6. secūrus : secure :: antīquus : _____antique_____

7. prīmus : prime :: sōlus : _____sole_____

8. historia : history :: glōria : _____glory_____

9. ōrātiō : oration :: resurrectiō : _____resurrection_____

10. fēlis : feline :: canis : _____canine_____

11. elephantus : elephantine :: equus : _____equine_____

12. mūris : murine :: anseris : _____anserine_____

© 1999 BJU Press. Reproduction prohibited.

CAPITULUM XVII

© 1999 BJU Press. Reproduction prohibited.

Activity A

Write *Vērum* for each true statement and *Falsum* for each false statement.

Falsum 1. Pyrrhus erat rēx Rōmānus.

Falsum 2. Pyrrhus vīvēbat° in paeninsulā Ītalicā.
[°live]

Vērum 3. Pyrrhus in Epirō prīmō vīvēbat.

Vērum 4. Pyrrhus Graecōs in proelium contrā° Rōmānōs dūcēbat.
[°against]

Vērum 5. Elephantī Graecōrum Rōmānōs terrēbant.

Falsum 6. Post duō proelia Rōmānī victōrēs erant.

Falsum 7. Post bellum contrā Rōmānōs, Pyrrhus et virī eius in Ītaliā remanēbant.

Vērum 8. Hodiē° victōria similis victōriae Pyrrhī nōn est vērē magna victōria.
[°today]

Activity B

Write the translation of each sentence.

1. Dēbētis, amīcī, dē populō Rōmānō cōgitāre°. (Cicero) _____
   You ought, friends, to think about the Roman people.
   [°think]

2. Valē, puella, iam° Catullus obdūrat°. (Catullus. He is breaking up with his girlfriend.)

   Goodbye, girl/girlfriend, now Catullus is determined.
   [°now; °is determined]

3. Salvē, bone amīce. (Terence) _____
   Greetings/Hello, good friend.

4. Sī° mē dūcēs, Mūsa,° corōnam° magnā cum laude° capiam. (Lucretius. *Magnā*

   modifies *laude.*) _____
   If you will lead me, Muse, I will take the crown with great praise.
   [°if; °Muse; °crown; °praise]

5. Salvē, O patria! (Plautus) _____

_____
Greetings, O fatherland/country!

6. O amice, vir bonus es. (Terence) _____

_____
O friend, you are a good man.

Activity C

Write these sentences in Latin. (A noun of address is not necessarily the first word of the sentence, especially in interrogative sentences.)

1. Good friend, God loves you. _____

_____
Amīce bone, Deus tē dīligit.

2. My brother, your story is true. _____

_____
Frāter mī, fabula tua est vēra.

3. Brave men, your victory is great. _____

_____
Virī fortēs, victōria tua est magna.

4. Claudius, we will stand with you. _____

_____
Claudī, cum tē / tēcum stābimus.

5. Are you also against me, Brutus? _____

_____
Esne quoque contrā mē, Brute?

© 1999 BJU Press. Reproduction prohibited.

Write the translation of each of these sentences taken from the Vulgate. Do not read the verses in your Bible until you have completed the activity. Obvious meanings are not given if the Latin words are spelled almost exactly like their English derivatives. (The sentence parts in brackets are translations, slightly modified to clarify the context.)

1. [Behold] angelus Dominī [appeared to Joseph in a dream saying] surge° et accipe°

   puerum et matrem eius et fuge° in Aegyptum. (Matthew 2:13) _____

   _____*[Behold] the angel of the Lord [appeared to Joseph*_____

   _____*in a dream saying] arise and take the child and his mother and flee into Egypt.*_____

   [°rise; °take; °flee]

2. [And he said to Peter and Andrew] venite post me. (Matthew 4:19) _____

   _____*[And he said to Peter and Andrew] come after me.*_____

3. Multī dīcent mihi in illā diē, Domine, Domine, [have we not prophesied] in nomine

   tuō? (Matthew 7:22) _____

   _____*Many will say to me in that day, Lord, Lord, [have we not prophesied] in thy/your name?*_____

4. [A certain man had] duōs filiōs, [and the younger one of them said to the father],

   pater da mihi portiōnem substantiae [which belongs to me]. (Luke 15:11-12)

   _____*[A certain man had] two sons, [and the younger one of them said to the father],*_____

   _____*father, give me / to me the portion of substance [which belongs to me].*_____

5. [The father said to the older son], fīlī, tū semper mēcum es et omnia mea tua sunt.

   (Luke 15:31) (The neuter plural ending *a* on *omnia* modifies the understood noun

   things.) _____

   _____*[The father said to the older son], son, you are always with me and all my things are yours.*_____

© 1999 BJU Press. Reproduction prohibited.

Write these sentences in Latin. Use the context (preceding sentences) to decide whether to use the singular or the plural form of imperative verbs if the sentence itself does not make the number of the verb clear.

1. Teacher, tell us a story. _____ *Magister, narrā nōbīs fabulam.* _____

2. Hear a story about a Roman leader. _____ *Audīte fabulam dē duce Rōmānō.* _____

3. Then, pupils, read from the book about Julius Caesar. _____

   _____ *Tum, discipulī, legite ā/ab (or ē/ex) librō dē Iuliō/Juliō Caesare.* _____

4. Teach us about the kings of Rome. _____ *Docē nōs dē rēgibus Rōmae.* _____

5. Boys and girls, learn the names of the kings. _____

   _____ *Puerī et puellae, discite nōmina rēgum.* _____

Choose from the list the appropriate noun to complete each sentence and write it in the blank. Use the correct inflection for the noun's function in the sentence.

argentum	caelum	manus	pēs
aurum	colonia	oculus	proelium
bellum	homo	ōs	terra

1. Prīmō Graecī in _____ *coloniīs* _____ in parte austrālī Ītaliae vīvēbant°.
   [°live]

2. Rōmānī elephantōs in _____ *bellō/proeliō/proeliīs* _____ contrā Pyrrhum timēbant.

3. _____ *Hominēs* _____ manūs, pedēs, oculōs, et ōs habent.

4. Propter _____ *pedēs* _____ homo ambulāre potest.

5. Propter _____ *oculōs* _____ homo vidēre potest.

6. Propter _____ *ōs* _____ homo dīcere potest.

7. Homo dīvēs° Rōmānus multum _____ *argentum* _____ et _____ *aurum* _____
   habēbat.
   [°rich]

8. Jupiter erat deus Rōmānus _____ *caelī/caelōrum* _____ et _____ *terrae* _____.

© 1999 BJU Press. Reproduction prohibited.

From the context and spelling, decide what is the Latin origin of each underlined English word. In the two blanks write the Latin word and its meaning. For each noun, write also the genitive ending; for each adjective, write also the gender forms. The derivatives are from words in both word lists in this chapter.

1. Several celestial bodies are named for Roman deities: for example, Jupiter, Venus, and Mars.

   _____*caelum, -ī*_____   _____*the sky, the heaven*_____

2. Scripture distinguishes Israel from the Gentiles (nations).

   _____*gēns, gentis*_____   _____*a people, a nation*_____

3. Pedestrians as well as drivers must obey traffic signals.

   _____*pēs, pedis*_____   _____*a foot*_____

4. A physician may prescribe ocular exercises for certain muscle problems.

   _____*oculus, -ī*_____   _____*an eye*_____

5. Historians are grateful for carefully preserved ancient manuscripts.

   _____*manus, -ūs*_____   _____*a hand*_____

6. The assigned reports are to be oral.

   _____*ōs, ōris*_____   _____*the mouth*_____

7. My report will be about Australia.

   _____*austrālis, -e*_____   _____*south*_____

8. The people of that peaceful country fear their bellicose neighbors.

   _____*bellum, -ī*_____   _____*war*_____

9. We tried a new method, but we finally reverted to our original method.

   _____*revertō, -ere*_____   _____*to turn back*_____

10. Because of the clarity of the article I read, my report was easy to prepare.

    _____*clārus, -a, -um*_____   _____*clear*_____

© 1999 BJU Press. Reproduction prohibited.

Activity H

This vocabulary review covers words from all the chapters you have studied thus far. Based on your understanding of the meaning of Latin words, answer each question.

1. The Latin word for "almost" is *paene*. The literal meaning of *peninsula,* then, is _____*"almost an island"*_____.

2. Is a *bellicose* nation peaceful or warlike? _____*warlike*_____

3. If we *revert* to old habits, do we overcome them or turn back to them? _____*We turn back to them.*_____

4. The word *Argentina* seems to have originated at the time when Magellan explored South America. He was impressed with the _____*silver*_____ ornaments worn by the Indians there.

5. Does a *resurgence* of interest in gold mining mean that interest had died down and then risen again or that there is a great lack of interest? _____ *It had died down and is risen again.*_____

6. If something is said to be *null* and void, does it have no meaning, a clear meaning, or a bad meaning? _____*no meaning*_____

7. Is the *sole* owner of something the first owner, the legal owner, or the only owner? _____*the only owner*_____

8. Most of the people who live in *agrarian* communities make their living by working in _____*fields / the field*_____.

9. A man with a *pugnacious* attitude is a man who likes to _____*fight*_____.

10. A *mortal* wound is one that results in _____*death*_____.

11. The *brevity* of the report was appreciated by the committee; it took a _____*short*_____ time to present the information.

12. A matter of *prime* importance should be dealt with _____*first*_____.

13. Two *aquatic* sports are _____*swimming*_____ and _____*boating*_____.

14. According to its motto, the United States Marine Corps is "Semper Fidelis." That means they are "Always _____*faithful*_____."

15. Our time and attention should not be given wholly to *mundane* matters—matters that deal only with this _____*world*_____.

© 1999 BJU Press. Reproduction prohibited.

CAPITULUM XVIII

Activity A

Complete each sentence by filling in the blank with the correct word or date.

1. The island at the "toe of the boot" of Italy is _____Sicily_____.

2. The city of Carthage was on the northern coast of _____Africa_____.

3. At the beginning of the First Punic War, Carthage did have and Rome did not have a strong _____navy_____.

4. The First Punic War was fought to determine who should control _____Sicily_____.

5. That war began in _____264_____ B.C. and ended in _____241_____ B.C.

6. The people of Carthage were _____Phoenicians_____, who had come from the city of Tyre.

7. During the First Punic War, the _____Carthaginians_____ used elephants, just as Pyrrhus had done earlier.

8. During the war the _____Romans_____ built a navy; their enemies already had a strong _____mercenary_____ navy.

9. After the war _____Rome_____ had control of Sicily, and Rome and Carthage were _____"friends"_____ ("friends"/"enemies").

Activity B

Write the English meaning of each word. (Here are meanings of verbs you have not been asked to learn: *manēre,* "to remain"; *legere,* "to read"; *dūcere,* "to lead.")

1. mansimus _____we have remained / we remained_____

2. lēgerō _____I will have read_____

3. lēgit _____he has read_____

4. dederās _____you (sing.) had given_____

5. cucurristis _____you (pl.) have run_____

6. dūxerint _____they will have led_____

7. timuērunt _____they have feared_____

© 1999 BJU Press. Reproduction prohibited.

8. vīderant _____ *they had seen*

9. ēgistī _____ *you (sing.) have done*

10. vīcistis _____ *you (pl.) have conquered*

Write each verb form in Latin. Be careful to mark all needed macrons.

1. we had stood _____ *steterāmus*

2. they have praised _____ *laudāvērunt*

3. you (pl.) will have defended _____ *dēfenderitis*

4. he had fallen _____ *ceciderat*

5. I will have built _____ *condiderō*

6. you (sing.) have loved _____ *dīlēxistī*

7. he had fled _____ *fūgerat*

8. he will have fled _____ *fūgerit*

9. he has fled _____ *fūgit*

10. he began _____ *incēpit*

Translate each sentence.

1. Dē Prīmō Punicō Bellō didicī. _____

   I have learned about the First Punic War.

2. Legistisne dē bellō inter° Rōmam et Carthāginem? _____

   Have you read about the war between Rome and Carthage?

   [°between, among]

3. Pyrrhus ex paeninsulā Ītaliā abierat° ante Prīmum Punicum Bellum. _____

   Pyrrhus had gone away from the Italian peninsula before the First Punic War.

   [°go away, leave]

4. Rōmānī Siciliam cēpērunt. _____

   The Romans have captured / captured Sicily.

5. Carthāgō Siciliam prius° habuerat. _____

   Carthage had held Sicily before.

   [°before]

© 1999 BJU Press. Reproduction prohibited.

© 1999 BJU Press. Reproduction prohibited.

Activity E

Write each sentence in Latin. You may need to look for some of the verbs in the lists on pages 254-55. In numbers 1 and 3, the words in brackets follow a word and a phrase you have not learned yet.

1. My grandfather had taught my father before [antequam] my father taught me.

   Avus meus patrem meum docuerat antequam pater meus mē docēbat/docuit.

2. My mother had taught us the Latin language before we learned the German language.

   Mater mea nōbīs linguam

   Latīnam docuerat antequam linguam Germānam discēbāmus/didicimus.

3. Our parents have made plans concerning our journey [itinere nostrō] to Europe.

   Parentēs nostrī consilia dē itinere nostrō ad Eurōpam fēcērunt.

4. We will have seen Germany before we will see Italy. _____

   Germāniam vīderimus antequam Ītaliam vidēbimus.

5. My grandmother has offered me books about Europe. _____

   Avia mea mihi librōs dē Eurōpā praebuit.

6. Have you seen my pictures [pictūrās] of Europe? _____

   Vīdistīne/Vīdistisne pictūrās meās Eurōpae?

Activity F

Write each word or phrase in Latin, giving both the singular and plural forms and all the possible gender forms. Remember that genitive and dative forms require no prepositions.

1. with whom _____ *cum quō / cum quibus*
2. for whom _____ *cui/quibus*
3. whom (DO) _____ *quem/quōs/quās*
4. whose _____ *cuius/quōrum/quārum*
5. who (S) _____ *quis/quī/quae*
6. what (S) _____ *quid/quae*
7. what (DO) _____ *quid/quae*
8. of what _____ *cuius/quōrum*
9. for what _____ *cui/quibus*
10. concerning what _____ *dē quō / dē quibus*

Write each question in English. In numbers 3 and 4 the pronoun subjects are used for emphasis. The subjects are clear from the verb endings.

1. Cui hoc° novum librum dabō? (Catullus) _____

   _____ *To whom will/shall I give this new book?* _____

   [°this]

2. Quī sunt bonī cīvēs? (Cicero) _____

   _____ *Who are good citizens?* _____

3. Quid vōs facere dēbētis? _____

   _____ *What ought you to do?* _____

4. Quid ego ēgī? _____

   _____ *What have I done?* _____

5. Quis erat prīmus imperātor° Rōmae? _____

   _____ *Who was the first emperor of Rome?* _____

   [°emperor]

6. Cuius frāter erat Remus? _____

   _____ *Whose brother was Remus?* _____

7. Quōrum vītae erant secūrae propter pastōrem? _____

   _____ *Whose lives were safe because of the shepherd?* _____

8. Quibus Pyrrhus in Ītaliā austrālī pugnābat? _____

   _____ *For whom did Pyrrhus fight in southern Italy?* _____

9. Dē quō Rōmānī et Carthāginiēnsēs pugnāre incēpērunt? ____ *Concerning what have the* ____

   ____ *Romans and the Carthaginians begun to fight / did the Romanls and the Carthāginians begin to fight?* ____

10. Erantne Rōma et Carthāgō "amīcae" post Prīmum Punicum Bellum? _____

    _____ *Were Rome and Carthage "friends" after the First Punic War?* _____

© 1999 BJU Press. Reproduction prohibited.

© 1999 BJU Press. Reproduction prohibited.

Activity H

Answer each question in Latin. Your answers may be brief. Be careful to use the correct case for each noun and adjective. The number in parentheses after each question tells you the number of the chapter that contains the answer.

1. Amulius erat frāter rēgis, Numitōris. Eratne Amulius bonus aut malus°? (11)

    malus
    _____
    [°bad, evil] **(Amulius was the brother of the king, Numitor. Was Amulius good or bad?)**

2. Cuius frāter erat Remus? (11)

    Romulī
    _____
    (Whose brother was Remus?)

3. Lupus et pastor geminīs cūram dābant. Quī erant geminī? (11)

    Rōmulus et Remus
    _____
    (The wolf and the shepherd gave care to the twins. Who were the twins?)

4. Quis contrā Aequōs pugnāvit et tum ad agrum redīvit°? (12)

    Cincinnātus
    _____
    [°returned] **(Who fought against the Aequians and then returned to the farm?)**

5. Quis in ponte stābat in proeliō contrā Etruscōs? (13)

    Horātius
    _____
    (Who stood / was standing on a bridge in the battle against the Etruscans?)

6. In fābulā dē anseribus, vītās quōrum—Rōmānōrum aut Gallōrum—anserēs

    servāvērunt? (16) _____*vītās Rōmānōrum / Rōmānōrum*_____
    (In the story about the geese, whose lives / the lives of whom—of the Romans or of the Gauls—did the geese save?)

7. Adiuvābatne Pyrrhus Graecōs aut Rōmānōs? (17)

    Graecōs
    _____
    (Did Pyrrhus help the Greeks or the Romans?)

8. Cuius victōria contrā Rōmānōs erat nōn vērē victōria magna? (17)

    victōria Pyrrhī
    _____
    (Whose victory against the Romans was not truly a great victory?)

Based on the information in this section, match each item in column 2 with the appropriate item in column 1. This is a challenge to distinguish ordinal numbers from cardinal numbers and the lunar calendar from the solar calendar. A helpful clue is the number of the word *mensis* and *mensēs*.

__D__ 1. lunar year	A. trēs	
__H__ 2. solar year	B. secundus rēx	
__B__ 3. Numa Pompilius	C. decimus mensis	
__E__ 4. March in lunar year	D. decem mensēs	
__G__ 5. March in solar year	E. prīmus mensis	
__C__ 6. December in lunar year	F. ordinal	
__I__ 7. December in solar year	G. tertius mensis	
__J__ 8. October in lunar year	H. duodecim mensēs	
__A__ 9. number of Punic wars	I. duodecimus mensis	
__F__ 10. numbers used to put things in order	J. octāvus mensis	

Match the words in column 2 with the related derivatives in column 1 by writing the letter in the correct blank.

__J__ i. initium	A. possibility	
__G__ ii. malus	B. decimal system	
__I__ iii. mare	C. sextet	
__H__ iv. esse	D. martial arts	
__A__ v. posse	E. octave	
__F__ vi. quārtus	F. quarter	
__B__ vii. decem	G. malicious	
__C__ viii. sextus	H. essential	
__E__ ix. octavus	I. marines	
__D__ x. Mars	J. initiation	

© 1999 BJU Press. Reproduction prohibited.

Complete each sentence by filling in an English word that explains the meaning of the underlined derivative. Then write the derivative's Latin origin. Number IV has two English derivatives with the same Latin origin.

I. The <u>United</u> States is a nation composed of fifty states that form

_____ *one—ūnus* _____ nation.

II. A meeting of the club had a <u>dual</u> purpose. The members discussed

_____ *two—duo* _____ important matters.

III. God is a <u>Trinity</u>: one God in _____ *three—trēs* _____ persons.

IV. A <u>quart</u> equals one- _____ *fourth—quārtus* _____ of a gallon; a <u>quarter</u> equals

one- _____ *fourth—quārtus* _____ of a dollar.

V. In a <u>quintet</u> _____ *five—quīnque/quintus* _____ musicians sing or play instruments.

VI. A <u>sextuple</u> is _____ *six—sex* _____ times larger than another number.

VII. A <u>septennial</u> event occurs once every _____ *seven—septem/septimus* _____ years.

VIII. An <u>octagon</u> has _____ *eight—octo/octāvus* _____ sides.

IX. In the Roman calendar, the <u>nones</u> was the _____ *ninth—nonus* _____ day

before the ides, which was the middle day of the month.

X. In 451-450 B.C., a group of Roman <u>decemvirs</u> wrote a code of laws. The work of

these _____ *ten men—decem virī* _____ was very important in the history of the

Roman republic.

XI. The <u>duodecimal</u> system is a number system that some people would prefer to the

decimal system. It is based on the number _____ *twelve—duodecim.* _____.

© 1999 BJU Press. Reproduction prohibited.

The derivatives in this activity are to help you learn the meanings of many of the verbs listed in this chapter. Some have not yet been included in lists you were required to learn, but they have been introduced in the lessons. Match the English words with their Latin origins by writing the correct letters in the blanks.

_E_	1. invincible	A.	able to be
_H_	2. legible	B.	able to be praised
_J_	3 audible	C.	able to act (move) easily
_I_	4. terrible	D.	able to be seen
_F_	5. stable	E.	not able to be conquered
_B_	6. laudable	F.	able to stand
_D_	7. visible	G.	able to be shown or displayed
_G_	8. ostensible	H.	able to be read
_A_	9. possible	I.	able to frighten
_C_	10. agile	J.	able to be heard

Activity M

In each blank, write the Latin word from which the underlined word came and write the English meaning of that word. If the Latin origin is a verb, give the infinitive form.

1. My friend's <u>initials</u> are R.H.K.

    initium—beginning

2. A sub<u>marine</u> was detected near the shore.

    mare—sea

3. The people were under the <u>domination</u> of a cruel dictator.

    dominātiō—mastery / irresponsible power

4. Sometimes a small army can <u>repel</u> a large army.

    repellere—to drive back

5. We should not <u>revert</u> to bad habits.

    revertere—to turn back

6. Parents and teachers <u>discipline</u> children to prepare them for adult life.

    discere—to learn

7. The <u>audience</u> applauded frequently during the man's speech.

    audīre—to hear

© 1999 BJU Press. Reproduction prohibited.

8. We ought not to <u>scribble</u> what we expect other people to read.

_____
                                    scrībere—to write

9. The <u>fugitives</u> were looking for a safe place to hide.

_____
                                    fugere—to flee

10. The boat left the shore and was quickly in the <u>current</u> of the river.

_____
                                    currere—to run

© 1999 BJU Press. Reproduction prohibited.

CAPITULUM XIX

Give brief Latin answers to these questions; they need not be complete sentences. The questions are based on the paragraphs you have just translated. Since there are no Latin words for *yes* and *no*, you may answer with *ita vērē* or *minimē* ("by no means").

1. Eratne exercitus Carthāginiensis in Hispāniā? _____ *Ita vērē.* _____

   (Was the Carthaginian army in Spain?)

2. Quis erat dux Rōmānus in Hispāniā tum? _____ *Scīpiō Maior* _____

   (Who was the Roman leader in Spain then?)

3. Quis elephantōs trāns Alpēs cēpit? _____ *Hannibal* _____

   (Who took elephants across the Alps?)

4. Hannibal et exercitus suus cum elephantīs Rōmānōs ferivērunt. Cui Poenī similēs

   fuērunt? _____ *Fulminī / Erant similēs fulminī.* _____ **(Hannibal and his army**

   with elephants struck the Romans. To what were the Carthaginians similar?)

5. Quis vītam Scīpiōnis Maiōris servāvit? _____ *Scīpiō Minor* _____

   (Who saved the life of Scipio the Elder?)

6. Quī in proeliō Cannīs° erant victōrēs? _____ *Poenī* _____

   [°at Cannae] **(Who were the victors in the battle at Cannae?)**

7. Quī in proeliō Capuae° erant victōrēs? _____ *Rōmānī* _____

   [°at Capua] **(Who were the victors in the battle at Capua?)**

8. Quōrum erat victōria ultima° Bellī Punicī Secundī Zamae°? _____ *Rōmānōrum*

   [°last; °at Zama] **(Whose was the final victory of the Second Punic War at Zama?)**

9. Eratne Zama in Africā aut in Ītaliā? _____ *In Africā / Erat in Africā.* _____

   (Was Zama in Africa or in Italy?)

© 1999 BJU Press. Reproduction prohibited.

Activity B

Translate each sentence. Use the word *own* to clarify the translation of any form of *suus, -a, -um.*

1. Hannibal ab suō patre odium° ad Rōmānōs didicit. _____

   Hannibal learned / has learned hatred toward the Romans from his own father.

   _____

   [°hatred]

2. Poenī in Ītaliam cum elephantīs suīs contendērunt. _____

   The Carthaginians hastened into Italy with their own elephants.

3. Rōmānī elephantōs eōrum timēbant. _____

   The Romans feared their elephants.

   _____

4. Poenī Rōmānōs in proeliō Cannīs vīcērunt. _____

   The Carthaginians defeated the Romans in the battle at Cannae.

   _____

5. Rōmānī Poenōs in proeliō Zamae vīcērunt. _____

   The Romans conquered the Carthaginians in the battle at Zama.

   _____

Activity C

Write the letter in each blank to show the correct meaning of the verb. You may need to refer to the Vocābulārium to check the conjugation of some verbs in order to determine the tense.

A 1. audītur
   A. He is heard.
   B. He was being heard
   C. He will be heard.

B 2. agēbātur
   A. It is done.
   B. It was being done.
   C. It will be done.

C 3. agētur
   A. It is done.
   B. It was being done.
   C. It will be done.

B 4. laudābāminī
   A. You are praised.
   B. You were being praised.
   C. You will be praised.

C 5. adiuvābimur
   A. We are helped.
   B. You were being helped.
   C. We will be helped.

C 6. capiēris
   A. You are captured.
   B. You were being captured.
   C. You will be captured.

C 7. docēbor
   A. I am taught.
   B. I was being taught.
   C. I will be taught.

C 8. dūcar
   A. I am led.
   B. I was being led.
   C. I will be led.

C 9. repellentur
   A. They are driven back.
   B. They were being driven back.
   C. They will be driven back.

A 10. videntur
   A. They are seen.
   B. They were being seen.
   C. They will be seen.

© 1999 BJU Press. Reproduction prohibited.

© 1999 BJU Press. Reproduction prohibited.

Activity D

Write each sentence in Latin, using only one word for each.

1. You are loved. _____ *Dīligeris. / Dīligiminī.*

2. You will be loved. _____ *Dīligēris. / Dīligēminī.*

3. It was being written. _____ *Scrībēbātur.*

4. It will be written. _____ *Scrībētur.*

5. It is written. _____ *Scrībitur.*

6. He is frightened. _____ *Terrētur.*

7. He will be frightened. _____ *Terrēbitur.*

8. She will be heard. _____ *Audiētur.*

9. She is heard. _____ *Audītur.*

10. They were being conquered. _____ *Vincēbantur.*

Activity E

Write each sentence in English. Some have verbs in the active voice and some in the passive.

1. Magistra docet. _____ *The teacher teaches.*

2. Lingua Latīna docēbātur. _____ *The Latin language was being taught.*

3. Lingua Latīna discētur. _____ *The Latin language will be learned.*

4. Discipulī laudābantur. _____ *The pupils were being praised.*

5. Legēturne liber ab° discipulīs? _____ *Will the book be read by the pupils?*
   [°by]

6. Librum legam. _____ *I will read the book.*

7. Dē historiā docēbor. _____ *I will be taught about history.*

8. Dux exercitum ducēbat. _____ *The military commander / general was leading the army.*

9. Exercitus in proelium ducētur. _____ *The army will be led into battle.*

10. Magnus exercitus timēbātur. _____ *The large/great army was feared / was being feared.*

Write each sentence in Latin.

11. Our country was being defended. _____ *Patria nostra dēfendēbātur.*

12. Will you (sing.) defend your country? _____ *Dēfendēsne patriam tuam?*

13. The city was being built. _____ *Urbs condēbātur.*

14. The men are being praised. _____ *Virī laudantur.*

15. Will you (pl.) also praise the men? _____ *Laudābitisne quoque virōs?*

Written exercises   **153**

Translate each sentence into a complete Latin sentence.

1. He praised° the work of one man. _____

   Opus unius virī laudāvit/laudābat.

   [°praise]

2. He gave one man all the money. _____

   Unī virō omnem pecūniam dedit.

3. We found the home of the two girls. _____

   Domum duārum puellārum invēnimus.

4. The two girls were with their mother. _____

   Duae puellae erant cum matre suā.

5. We gave them two books. _____

   Eīs duōs librōs dedimus.

6. The parents have two daughters. _____

   Parentēs fīliās duās habent.

7. Do you have three names? _____

   Habēsne/Habētisne nōmina tria?

8. The names of the three boys are Quintus, Marcus, and Flavius. _____

   Nōmina trium puerōrum sunt Quintus, Marcus, et Flavius.

9. The Carthaginian general led one thousand soldiers. _____

   Dux Poenus/Carthaginiensis unum mille mīlitēs dūcēbat/dūxit.

10. The Roman general led thousands of soldiers. _____

    Dux Rōmānus milia mīlitum dūcēbat/dūxit.

© 1999 BJU Press. Reproduction prohibited.

Activity G

Translate each phrase into Latin.

1. first day (subject) _____ *diēs prīmus/prīma* _____

2. two hands (direct object) _____ *duās manūs* _____

3. in the third year (time when) _____ *annō tertiō* _____

4. to the fourth son (indirect object) _____ *fīliō quārtō* _____

5. with five soldiers _____ *cum quinque militibus* _____

6. the sixth time (subject) _____ *tempus sextum* _____

7. of seven things _____ *septem rērum* _____

8. for eight senators (indirect object) _____ *octō senātōribus* _____

9. in nine towns _____ *in novem oppidīs* _____

10. the tenth victory (direct object) _____ *victōriam decimam* _____

Activity H

Translate each sentence or Latin portion of a sentence. If the sentence is in quotation marks, it is a direct quotation. If it is not in quotation marks, it is a paraphrase of the verse (that is, the same thought in slightly different wording to make it easier to translate.)

1. [Cornelius, a Roman centurion,] vīdit angelum quasi° hōrā° nōnā. (Acts 10:3)

    [Cornelius, a Roman centurion,] saw an angel at about / about the ninth hour.

    [°about; °hour]

2. [Peter went up onto the housetop to pray] "circā° hōram sextam." (Acts 10:9)

    [Peter went up onto the housetop to pray] "about/around the sixth hour."

    [°about, around]

3. [While Peter was thinking about the vision he had just seen,] "dīxit Spiritus eī ecce°

    virī trēs quaerunt° tē." (Acts 10:19) _____ *[While Peter was thinking about the vision*

    he had just seen,] "the Spirit said to him, behold, three men seek / are seeking you."

    [°behold! see!; °seek]

4. Eum Deus suscitāvit° tertiā diē°. (Acts 10:40) _____

    God raised him / made him to rise the third day / on the third day.

    [°raised; °day]

5. [Immediately] trēs virī erant in domō°. (Acts 11:11) _____

    [Immediately] three men were in the house.

    [°house]

© 1999 BJU Press. Reproduction prohibited.

Written exercises

6. Sex frātrēs mēcum venērunt. (Acts 11:12) _____

    Six brothers came with me.

7. [In the same night Peter was sleeping] inter duōs mīlitēs, [bound by] catēnīs° duābus.

    (Acts 12:6) _____

    [In the same night Peter was sleeping] between two soldiers, [bound by] two chains.

    [°chains]

8. "Unus diēs apud° Dominum *est* sicut° mille annī et mille annī *sunt* sicut diēs unus."

    (II Peter 3:8) _____

    "One day is with the Lord as a thousand years and a thousand years are as one day."

    [°with; °as]

9. "Milia milium ministrābant° eī." (Daniel 7:10) _____

    "Thousands of thousands were ministering to / serving him."

    [°minister, serve]

Activity I

Write **R** if the underlined word is a relative pronoun; write **I** if it is an interrogative pronoun.

____R____ 1. Puerī <u>quibus</u> librōs dedistī discipulī meī sunt.

    (The boys to whom you gave the books are my pupils.)

____R____ 2. Librī <u>quōs</u> mihi dedit sunt novī.

    (The books which he gave me are new.)

____I____ 3. <u>Quōrum</u> magistra est Fulvia?

    (Whose teacher is Fulvia?)

____R____ 4. Opus <u>quod</u> fēcī erat dūrum.

    (The work which I did was hard.)

____I____ 5. <u>Quid</u> est nōmen frātris tuī?

    (What is the name of your brother / your brother's name?)

© 1999 BJU Press. Reproduction prohibited.

Translate each sentence.

1. Dux quī mīlitēs Rōmānōs dūcēbat erat Scīpio Maior. _____

   The military leader / general who was leading / led the Roman soldiers was Scipio the Elder.

2. Ducēs quī mīlitēs Poenōs ducēbant erant Hannibal et Hasdrubal. _____

   The generals who led the Carthaginians were Hannibal and Hasdrubal.

3. Dux cuius vītam Scīpio Minor servāvit erat Scīpio Maior. _____

   The general whose life Scipio the Younger saved was Scipio the Elder.

4. Ducēs quōrum mīlitēs elephantōs timēbant erant ducēs Rōmānī. _____

   The generals whose soldiers feared the elephants were Roman generals.

5. Urbs cui Hannibal magnum odium° habēbat erat Rōma. _____

   The city for which Hannibal had great hatred was Rome.

   [°hatred]

6. Virī quibus Hannibal magnum odium habēbat erant Rōmānī. _____

   The men for whom Hannibal had great hatred were the Romans.

7. Urbs quam Scīpio dēfendēbat erat Rōma. _____

   The city which Scipio was defending / defended was Rome.

8. Elephantī quōs Hannibal ad Ītaliam ducēbat Rōmanos terrebat. _____

   The elephants which Hannibal led to Italy terrified the Romans.

9. Carthāgō erat urbs ex quā Hannibal vēnit. _____

   Carthage was the city from which Hannibal came.

10. Cannae, Capua, et Zama erant trēs urbēs ad quās proelia pugnābantur. _____

    Cannae, Capua, and Zama were three cities near/at which battles were fought.

© 1999 BJU Press. Reproduction prohibited.

Activity K

Complete each comparison by filling in the blank with the correct English word.

1. vīsus : vision :: mansus : _____ *mansion* _____
2. actus : act :: intentus : _____ *intent* _____
3. creditus : credit :: scriptus : _____ *script* _____
4. legere : legible :: credere : _____ *credible* _____
5. laudāre : laudable :: stāre : _____ *stable* _____
6. constructus : constructive :: fugitus : _____ *fugitive* _____
7. cursus : cursive :: captus : _____ *captive* _____
8. dictus : diction :: audītus : _____ *audition* _____
9. actus : action :: intentus : _____ *intention* _____
10. scīre : science :: convenīre : _____ *convenience* _____

Activity L

Complete each comparison by filling in the blank with the correct Latin word.

1. domination : dominātiōnis :: investigation : _____ *investigātiōnis* _____
2. oration : orātiōnis :: resurrection : _____ *resurrectiōnis* _____
3. secure : sēcūrus :: pure : _____ *pūrus* _____
4. prime : prīmus :: sole : _____ *sōlus* _____
5. tribune : tribunus :: tribe : _____ *tribus* _____
6. public : publicus :: secret : _____ *sēcrētus* _____
7. Rome : Rōma :: Europe : _____ *Eurōpa* _____
8. pork : porcus :: trunk : _____ *truncus* _____
9. colony : colōnia :: victory : _____ *victōria* _____
10. brevity : brevis :: facility : _____ *facilis* _____
11. eternity : aeternus :: unity : _____ *ūnus* _____
12. ascend : ascendere :: contend : _____ *contendere* _____

© 1999 BJU Press. Reproduction prohibited.

Match each sentence or phrase quoted from a Roman writer with its translation. One translation will not be used. You may not know all the words, but you have sufficient context clues and helps in the translations to learn the meaning of each sentence and phrase.

_A_ 1. Divina natura dedit agros; ars humana aedificavit urbes.

_G_ 2. Omnia mors aequat.

_E_ 3. Necessitas non habet legem.

_I_ 4. Magna est veritas et praevalet.

_D_ 5. Mens sana in corpore sano

_F_ 6. Aut amat aut odit mulier; nihil est tertium.

_J_ 7. Bis vincit qui se vincit in victoria.

_C_ 8. Carpe diem.

_K_ 9. O tempora, O mores!

_B_ 10. Rara avis

A. Divine nature gave the fields; human art built the cities.

B. Rare bird

C. Seize the day.

D. A sound mind in a sound body

E. Necessity does not have a law.

F. A woman either loves or hates; nothing is third.

G. Death makes all things equal.

H. All art is an imitation of nature.

I. Great is truth and it prevails.

J. He conquers twice who conquers himself in victory.

K. O the times, O the customs!

© 1999 BJU Press. Reproduction prohibited.

In each blank, write the letter for the matching meaning. Some definitions include more than the original Latin meanings because through use in our language some words have become more specific in their meanings.

_D_ 1. invade

_I_ 2. invasion

_A_ 3. major

_H_ 4. minor

_J_ 5. transition

_E_ 6. fulminate

_C_ 7. vulnerable

_F_ 8. auxiliary

_G_ 9. revert

_B_ 10. final

A. larger, greater

B. occurring at the end, forming the end

C. susceptible to being wounded

D. to go in by force

E. to explode thunderously or with a vivid flash

F. giving assistance, helping

G. to turn back

H. smaller, lesser

I. the act of entering by force

J. the act of going across from one place, subject, or form to another

© 1999 BJU Press. Reproduction prohibited.

CAPITULUM XX

Activity A

Complete each sentence by filling in the correct word(s) or date.

1. The Roman general named _____*Regulus*_____ was captured by the Carthaginians during the First Punic War.

2. He proved his loyalty to _____*Rome*_____ by persuading the _____*senate*_____ to continue the war, and he proved his honesty to _____*Carthage*_____ by returning and accepting a cruel death.

3. Between the end of the Second Punic War in the year _____*201 B.C.*_____ and the beginning of the Third Punic War in the year _____*149 B.C.*_____, Rome fought four wars against the country of _____*Macedonia*_____.

4. The Third Punic War ended in the year _____*146 B.C.*_____

5. Carthage did not keep the promise she had made to Rome at the end of the _____*Second*_____ Punic War. Instead, she secretly armed her _____*ships*_____ again for war.

6. A Roman senator named _____*Cato*_____ said to the senate again and again, _____*"Carthage must be destroyed."*_____

7. When Rome tried to discuss with Carthage the pact that the Carthaginians had broken, Carthage treated Rome's delegates in a/an _____*rude/insolent*_____ manner.

8. When Rome declared war and Carthage surrendered, Carthage did not hand over all her _____*weapons*_____.

9. During the brief war, a Carthaginian general named _____*Hasdrubal*_____ defended his city.

10. However, Carthage was completely destroyed by _____*flames*_____.

© 1999 BJU Press. Reproduction prohibited.

Translate each sentence.

1. Urbēs Rōmae et Carthāginis erant nōn amīcae. _____
   The cities of Rome and Carthage were not friends/friendly.

2. Rōmānī et Poenī tria bella pugnābant. _____
   The Romans and the Carthaginians fought three wars.

3. In Prīmō, Secundō, et Tertiō Punicō Bellō, Rōmānī Poenōs vīcērunt. _____
   In the First, the Second, and the Third Punic War, the Romans conquered the Carthaginians.

4. Cato erat senātor Rōmānus, et Hasdrubal erat dux Carthāginiensis. _____
   Cato was a Roman senator, and Hasdrubal was a Carthaginian general.

5. In Tertiō Punicō Bellō uxor et līberī Hasdrubalis periērunt in flammīs. _____
   In the Third Punic War the wife and children of Hasdrubal perished in the flames.

6. Tertia victōria Rōmae contrā Carthāginem erat finis urbis Carthāginis. _____ *The third*
   victory of Rome / Rome's third victory against Carthage was the end of the city of Carthage.

Translate each sentence. Be careful to make each verb accurate in person, number, tense, and voice.

1. Fābula narrātur. _____ *The story is told.*

2. Fābula audiētur. _____ *The story will be heard.*

3. Verba dīcēbantur. _____ *The words were spoken / were being spoken.*

4. Patria dēfendēbatur. _____ *The country / native land was defended / was being defended.*

5. Opus factum est. _____ *The work was done / has been done.*

6. Proelium pugnātum erat. _____ *The battle had been fought.*

7. Carthāgō victa erit. _____ *Carthage will have been conquered.*

8. Pecūnia data est. _____ *The money has been given / was given.*

9. Tū dīligeris. _____ *You are loved.*

10. Ego vocābar. _____ *I was called / was being called.*

11. Vocābāminīne vōs? _____ *Were you called? / Were you being called?*

12. Vocāta sum. _____ *I have been called / was called.*

13. Ductī erant. _____ *They / The men had been led.*

14. Historia Rōmae scripta est. _____ *The history of Rome has been written / was written.*

15. Liber inveniētur. _____ *The book will be found.*

© 1999 BJU Press. Reproduction prohibited.

After each sentence, give (1) the word that names the receiver of action and (2) the function of that word. Then translate the sentence on the second line.

1a. Carthāgō nāvēs armāvit. _____nāvēs_____ _____direct object_____

_____Carthage has armed / armed the ships._____

1b. Nāvēs armātae sunt. _____Nāvēs_____ _____subject_____

_____The ships have been / were armed._____

2a. Carthāgō prōmissiōnem fēcerat. _____prōmissiōnem_____ _____direct object_____

_____Carthage had made a promise._____

2b. Prōmissiō facta erat. _____Prōmissiō_____ _____subject_____

_____A promise had been made._____

3a. Rōma lēgātōs mīsit. _____lēgātōs_____ _____direct object_____

_____Rome has sent / sent delegates/deputies._____

3b. Lēgātī mīsī sunt. _____Lēgātī_____ _____subject_____

_____Delegates have been / were sent._____

4a. Senātus Rōmānus bellum dēnuntiāvit. _____bellum_____ _____direct object_____

_____The Roman senate has declared / declared war._____

4b. Bellum dēnuntiātum est. _____bellum_____ _____subject_____

_____War has been / was declared._____

5a. Rōmānī omnia arma postulāvērunt. _____arma_____ _____direct object_____

_____The Romans have demanded / demanded all the arms/weapons._____

5b. Omnia arma postulāta sunt. _____arma_____ _____subject_____

_____All arms have been / were demanded._____

6a. Poenī multa arma dedidērunt. _____arma_____ _____direct object_____

_____The Carthaginians have surrendered / surrendered many arms/weapons._____

6b. Multa arma dedita sunt. _____arma_____ _____subject_____

_____Many weapons have been / were surrendered._____

7a. Mīlitēs Rōmānī urbem circumclusērunt. _____urbem_____ _____direct object_____

_____Roman soldiers have surrounded / surrounded the city._____

7b. Urbs circumclūsa est. _____Urbs_____ _____subject_____

_____The city has been / was surrounded._____

© 1999 BJU Press. Reproduction prohibited.

8a. Hasdrubal urbem dēfendēbat. ___*urbem*___ ___direct object___

Hasdrubal was defending / defended the city.

8b. Urbs dēfendēbātur. ___*Urbs*___ ___subject___

The city was being / was defended.

Activity E

Name the verb in each sentence, identify its four properties, and then translate the sentence. In number 3, supply the noun *things,* which is understood by the neuter plural adjective. Notice that in number 5 the Latin auxiliary precedes the main verb.

1. Probitās° laudātur. (Juvenal)

   Verb ___*laudātur*___; Number ___*Singular*___; Person ___*Third*___;

   Tense ___*Present*___; Voice ___*Passive*___

   Honesty/Uprightness is praised.

   [°honesty, uprightness]

2. Carmina° nova cantō. (Horace)

   Verb ___*cantō*___; Number ___*Singular*___; Person ___*First*___;

   Tense ___*Present*___; Voice ___*Active*___

   I sing new songs.

   [°a song, a poem]

3. Omnia mūtantur°. (Ovid)

   Verb ___*mutantur*___; Number ___*Plural*___; Person ___*Third*___;

   Tense ___*Present*___; Voice ___*Passive*___

   All things are changed / are being changed.

   [°change]

4. Mea puella° passerem° suum amābat°. (Catullus)

   Verb ___*amābat*___; Number ___*Singular*___; Person ___*Third*___;

   Tense ___*Imperfect*___; Voice ___*Active*___

   My girlfriend loved her sparrow.

   [°girlfriend; °sparrow; °love]

5. Senex° est līberātus°. (Cicero)

   Verb ___*est līberātus*___; Number ___*Singular*___; Person ___*Third*___;

   Tense ___*Present perfect*___; Voice ___*Passive*___

   The old man was set free / has been set free.

   [°an old man or woman; °set free]

© 1999 BJU Press. Reproduction prohibited.

Translate each sentence. The meanings of some new words are not given because the context and the similarity to English derivatives make the meanings obvious. Guess the meanings of those words. In number 5 you may use "by" to translate the preposition *in*.

1. Et dīcēbat eīs, vōbīs datum est mysterium regnī Deī. (Mark 4:11)

   And he said to them, the mystery of the kingdom of God has been given to you /

   to you has been given the mystery of the kingdom of God.

2. Missus est angelus Gabrihel a Deō in cīvitātem° Galilaeae. (Luke 1:26)

   The angel Gabriel was sent by God into a city of Galilee.

   [°city]

3. Vocābitur Fīlius Deī. (Luke 1:35)

   He will be called the Son of God. / The Son of God will be called.

   (The second is a possible translation without a context.)

4. Et tū, puer, prophēta Altissimī° vocāberis. (Luke 1:76)

   And you/thou, boy/child, will be called the prophet of the Highest.

   [°the Highest]

5. Scriptum est nōn in pane° solō vīvet homo sed in omnī verbō quod procedit° dē ore° Deī. (Matthew 4:4)

   It has been written man shall not live

   by bread alone but by every word which proceeds from the mouth of God.

   [°bread; °proceeds; °mouth]

© 1999 BJU Press. Reproduction prohibited.

Activity G

These sentences taken from Activity D are in the passive voice and do not indicate the actor(s). In sentences 5a-8a the actors are stated. Rewrite each Latin sentence, adding the actor in an ablative-of-agent phrase.

5b. Omnia arma postulāta sunt. _____

         Omnia arma ā Rōmānīs postulāta sunt.

6b. Multa arma dedita sunt. _____

         Multa arma ā Poenīs dedita sunt.

7b. Urbs circumclusa est. _____

         Urbs ā mīlitibus Rōmānīs circumclusa est.

8b. Urbs dēfendēbātur. _____

         Urbs ab Hasdrubale dēfendēbātur.

Activity H

Write these sentences in Latin. They are similar to the ones in Activity C, but the verbs in most of these sentences differ in tense from those verbs.

1. The story has been told by my father. _____

         Fabula ā patre meō narrāta est.

2. The words had been spoken by the general. _____

         Verba ā duce dicta erant.

3. The country is being defended by the soldiers. _____

         Patria ā mīlitibus defenditur.

4. The work has been done by his help. _____

         Opus auxiliō eius factum est.

5. The family of Hasdrubal was killed by flames. _____

         Familia Hasdrubalis flammīs necāta est.

6. The history of Rome was written by Titus Livius. _____

         Historia Rōmae ā Titō Liviō scripta est.

7. The book was written with a stilus. _____

         Liber stilō scriptus est.

© 1999 BJU Press. Reproduction prohibited.

© 1999 BJU Press. Reproduction prohibited.

Activity I

Translate each question.

1. In quō exercitū erat Hasdrubal? _____

   _____ *In what/which army was Hasdrubal?* _____

2. Cuius pater erat Hamilcar? _____

   _____ *Whose father was Hamilcar?* _____

3. In quā patriā est Tiber flūmen? _____

   _____ *In what country is the Tiber river / river Tiber?* _____

4. Quae urbs bella tria contrā Rōmam pugnābat? _____

   _____ *What city fought three wars against Rome?* _____

5. Quī erant quinque ducēs clārī? _____

   _____ *Who were five famous generals?* _____

6. In quō bellō Carthāgō dēstructa est? _____

   _____ *In what/which war was Carthage destroyed?* _____

Activity J

Translate each sentence and then write in the blank *A* (interrogative pronoun), *B* (interrogative adjective), or *C* (relative pronoun).

____*A*____ 1. Quid ego ēgī? (Terence) _____ *What have I done?* _____

____*B*____ 2. In quā urbe vīvimus°? (Cicero) _____ *In what city do we live?* _____
   [°live]

____*A*____ 3. Quem nunc amābis°? (Catullus) _____ *Whom will you now love?* _____
   [°love]

____*C*____ 4. Dionysius, dē quō ante° dīxī, ad Siciliam nāvigābat°. (Cicero) _____

   _____ *Dionysius, concerning whom I spoke / have spoken before, was sailing to Sicily.* _____
   [°before; °sail]

____*B*____ 5. In quō perīculō sum? (Terence) _____ *In what danger am I?* _____

____*A*____ 6. Quī sunt bonī cīvēs°? (Cicero) _____ *Who are good citizens?* _____
   [°citizen]

____*B*____ 7. Quae vīta tibi manet°? (Catullus) _____ *What life remains for you?* _____
   [°remain]

In each sentence a word or part of a word is underlined. In the blank, write the English meaning of that Latin source word.

1. God is im<u>mut</u>able. _____ *to change* _____

2. Obeying the law and voting are <u>civic</u> duties. _____ *citizen* _____

3. The principal will accept a <u>valid</u> excuse for tardiness. _____ *strong/powerful* _____

4. The teacher kindly re<u>iterated</u> the assignment. _____ *again* _____

5. A <u>navi</u>gable river is wide and deep. _____ *to sail* _____

6. To end the war, the two nations signed a <u>pact</u>. _____ *treaty/agreement* _____

7. After the war the prisoners were <u>liberated</u>. _____ *to set free* _____

8. The <u>navy</u> then had to repair the damage done. _____ *ship* _____

9. The <u>flammable</u> materials had to be replaced. _____ *flame* _____

10. The <u>merchant</u> ships had not been damaged. _____ *trade/business* _____

11. Trade between the nations re<u>vived</u>. _____ *to live* _____

12. In the sixteenth century the Spanish <u>Armada</u> was a powerful navy. _____ *to arm / weapons* _____

13. An <u>insolent</u> attitude is disrespectful. _____ *rude/ill-mannered* _____

14. An <u>adverse</u> opinion can be stated respectfully. _____ *against* _____

15. We admired the boy's <u>vim</u>, vigor, and vitality. _____ *strength/power* _____

The phrases (and abbreviations for which some phrases stand) are in common English use. The vocabulary and grammar in each has been covered in Chapters 1-20. Translate each one. (Macrons are not used because these are English phrases.)

1. quod vide, q.v. (used in cross-references) _____ *which see* _____

2. id est, i.e. _____ *it is / that is* _____

3. ab initio _____ *from the beginning* _____

4. ad finem _____ *to the end* _____

5. ars longa, vita brevis _____ *art [is] long, life [is] short* _____

6. post mortem _____ *after death* _____

7. ex tempore (freely translated "without preparation") _____ *from the time* _____

8. prima facie (freely translated "before closer inspection") _____ *at first face/appearance* _____

9. de novo _____ *from new / from a new thing* _____

10. ex libris [of the person named] (used to show ownership) _____ *from the books* _____

© 1999 BJU Press. Reproduction prohibited.

This activity reviews vocabulary covered in Chapters 1-20. Match the English meanings with the Latin words. Not all the words in column 2 will be used.

Part 1

D	1. tōtus, -a, -um	A. tribe
I	2. timeō, -ēre, timuī	B. across
G	3. terra, -ae	C. time
A	4. tribus, -ī	D. whole
K	5. truncus, -ī	E. third
J	6. tredecim	F. then
B	7. trāns	G. land
E	8. tertius	H. now
C	9. tempus, -oris	I. to fear
F	10. tum	J. thirteen
		K. trunk

Part 2

B	1. vērus, -a, -um	A. life
H	2. via, -ae	B. true
I	3. vigintī	C. wound
K	4. vitium, -iī/ī	D. wish, will
A	5. vīta, -ae	E. common people
J	6. vīvus, -a, -um	F. to see
E	7. vulgus, -ī	G. to call
C	8. vulnus, -eris	H. road, way
G	9. vocō (1)	I. twenty
D	10. voluntās, -tātis	J. living
		K. fault

© 1999 BJU Press. Reproduction prohibited.

CAPITULUM XXI

Answer each question in Latin. If your answer is brief, use the inflections you would in a complete sentence. In number 1 you will see that a genitive-case noun can modify another genitive-case noun. For the meaning of any unfamiliar Latin word, make a reasonable guess based on a related English word.

1. Quid erat nōmen frātrī Tiberiī Gracchī? _____ *Gaius / Gaius Gracchus* _____

   (What was the name of Tiberius Gracchus's brother?)

2. Quis erat māter Tiberiī et Gaiī? _____ *Cornēlia* _____

   (Who was the mother of Tiberius and Gaius?)

3. Quod nōmen fīliīs Cornēliae datum est? _____ *gemmae Cornēliae* _____

   (What name was given to the sons of Cornelia?)

4. Eratne familia Gracchōrum plēbēia aut patricia? _____ *patricia* _____

   (Was the family of the Gracchi plebeian or patrician?)

5. Optāvēruntne frātrēs corrigere iniustitiās? _____ *Ita vērē / Optāvērunt corrigere iniustitiās.* _____

   (Did the brothers wish to correct injustices?)

6. Pauperēsne aut dīvitēs familiae agrōs possidēbant? _____ *dīvitēs* _____

   (Did poor or rich families possess the fields/farms?)

7. Erantne Tiberius et Gaius Gracchus tribūnī patriciī aut tribūnī plēbis?

   _____ *Erant tribūnī patriciī.* _____

   (Were Tiberius and Gaius Gracchus patrician tribunes or tribunes of the plebs?)

8. Optāvēruntne senātōrēs mūtātiōnēs? _____ *Nōn optāvērunt mūtātiōnēs.* _____

   (Did the senators wish/want changes?)

9. Sectātōrēsne aut inimīcī Tiberiī Gracchī eum in flūmen Tiberim iēcit? _____ *Inimīcī* _____

   (Did followers or enemies of Tiberius Gracchus throw him into the Tiber river?)

10. Quis erat similis Tiberiō Gracchō? _____ *Gaius Gracchus / Frāter suus* _____

    (Who was similar to Tiberius Gracchus?)

© 1999 BJU Press. Reproduction prohibited.

11. Quī ex inimīcīs Gaiī Gracchī fūgērunt? _____*"amīcī" Gaiī Gracchī*_____

   (Who fled from the enemies of Gaius Gracchus?)

12. Cur° labōrēs Gracchōrum frātrum nōn Rōmam adiūvunt? _____

   ___*Quod et dīvitēs Rōmānī et pauperēs Rōmānī erant avārī.*___

   [°why] **(Why did the labors of the Gracchi brothers not help Rome?)**

Activity B

In each blank write the letter for the matching term. One term will be used three times.

___F___ 1. tribūnī patriciī   A. Cornēlia

___A___ 2. mater Gracchōrum frātrum   B. Via Appia

___E___ 3. avus Gracchōrum frātrum   C. Rōmānī dīvitēs et pauperēs

___F___ 4. fīliī parentum clārōrum   D. familia Gracchōrum frātrum

___F___ 5. amīcī pauperum Rōmānōrum   E. Scīpio Africānus

___B___ 6. via antīqua Rōmāna   F. Tiberius et Gaius

___D___ 7. familia patricia

___C___ 8. Rōmānī avārī

Activity C

Write each phrase in Latin. Remember that *is, ea, id* can be used to translate either *this* or *that*. Include a form of each of these pronouns at least once: *is, ea, id; hic, haec, hoc; ille, illa, illud; iste, ista, istud.* An English phrase may contain a noun that in Latin is understood because of the gender and number of the inflection; if so, you may omit or include that noun in your answer. Nearly always the word for *thing* is omitted in Latin; it is understood from the neuter adjective inflection.

1. with those boys _____*cum (puerīs) illīs/eīs*_____

2. of those bad boys _____*(puerōrum) istōrum*_____

3. for him _____*eī/huic/illī/istī*_____

4. for them _____*eīs/hīs/illīs/istīs*_____

5. with her _____*cum eā/hāc/illā/istā*_____

6. with these girls _____*cum puellīs hīs*_____

7. all those things (subject or direct object) _____*omnia illa/ista/ea*_____

8. all those girls (subject) _____*omnēs (puellae) illae/istae/eae*_____

9. all these boys (subject) _____*omnēs (puerī) hī/eī*_____

10. this thing (subject or direct object) _____*hoc/id*_____

© 1999 BJU Press. Reproduction prohibited.

© 1999 BJU Press. Reproduction prohibited.

Here are selections from the Gospel of John as found in the Vulgate. The macrons, which Jerome did not use, are supplied here. Each sentence contains one or more of the pronouns that you have studied. Translate each sentence without looking at an English translation of the Bible. Some new words are not defined because the meanings are obvious.

1. Et hoc est testimōnium Iohānnis. (1:19) _____

   And this is the testimony of John.

2. Respondit eīs Iohannes dīcēns° ego baptizō in aquā. (1:26) _____

   John responded to them saying I baptize in water.

   [°saying]

3. Haec in Bethaniā facta sunt trāns Iordanen. (1:28) _____

   These things were done in Bethany across the Jordan.

4. Hic est Fīlius Deī. (1:34) _____

   This is the Son of God.

5. Quid quaeritis°? (1:38) _____

   What are you seeking? / What do you seek?

   [°seek]

6. Ecce vērē Israhelita in quō dolus° non est. (1:47) _____

   Behold truly an Israelite in whom is not deceit/guile.

   [°deceit, guile]

7. Domine dā mihi hanc aquam. (4:15) _____

   Lord, give me / to me this water.

8. Patrēs nostrī in monte° hōc adōrāvērunt°. (4:20) _____

   Our fathers worshiped in/on this mountain.

   [°mountain; °worshiped]

9. Mulier . . . dīcit illīs hominibus, venīte vidēte hominem quī dīxit mihi omnia

   quaecumque° fēcī. (4:28-29) _____ *The woman says to those men,*

   come see the man who said to / told me all things whatsoever I have done.

   [°whatsoever]

10. Quis est ille homo quī dīxit tibi [take up your bed and walk]? (5:12) _____

    Who is that man who said to you [take up your bed and walk]?

11. Multitūdō maxima° vēnit ad eum. (6:5) _____

    A very great multitude came to him.

    [°very great]

12. Dīxērunt ergo° ad eum, Domine, semper° da nobis panem hunc. (6:34) _____

_____ **They said therefore to him, Lord, always give us this bread.** _____

[°therefore; °always]

13. Dīxit autem° eīs Iēsus ego sum panis vītae. (6:35) _____

_____ **Jesus moreover / Moreover Jesus said to them I am the bread of life.** _____

[°moreover]

© 1999 BJU Press. Reproduction prohibited.

Translate each sentence. Do not read these verses in your Bible while you are doing the activity.

The sentences are taken from Beza's translation of the Gospel of Matthew. This translation was made in the seventeenth century. By that time the letter *j* had replaced the letter *i* (1) at the beginning of any word having a vowel as the second letter and (2) between vowels. Ancient Latin did not have the letter *j*.

Remember that three or four periods (ellipsis marks) indicate omitted parts of sentences. The word *one* is supplied in number 4 to show that *habēns* modifies an understood word. The italicized personal pronoun in number 9 is not in the original Greek sentence; it was supplied by Beza to make the subject clear.

1. Vōs estis sal° terrae. (5:13) _____

   You/Ye are the salt of the earth.

   [°salt]

2. Ego vērō° dīcō vōbīs . . . (5:32) _____

   I truly say to you . . .

   [°truly]

3. Sed quaerite° prīmō regnum Deī, et justitiam° ejus. . . . (6:33) _____

   But seek first the kingdom of God and his righteousness. . . .

   [°seek; °righteousness]

4. Docēbat . . . eōs ut° [*one*] habēns auctoritātem°. . . . (7:29) _____

   He was teaching / taught them as [one] having authority. . . .

   [°as; °authority]

5. Quālis est iste . . . ? (8:27) _____

   What kind (of man) is that / that one / he . . .?

6. Et ecce, ruit° totus° ille grex° porcōrum ē praecipitiō° in mare. . . . (8:32) _____

   And behold, that whole herd of pigs rushed from the precipice into the sea. . . .

   [°rushed; °whole; °herd; °precipice]

7. Et exiit° haec fāma° in tōtam illam regiōnem. (9:26) _____

   And this report went forth into that whole region.

   [°went out, went forth; °report, fame]

8. Hōs duodecim mīsit Jesus. (10:5) _____

   Jesus sent these twelve (men).

9. Tunc° dīcit hominī illī, Protende° manum tuam. Et *is* extendit°. (12:13) _____

   Then he says to that man, Stretch forth your/thy hand. And he stretched it out.

   [°then; °stretch forth; °stretch out]

10. Nōnne iste est fīlius ille Davidis? (12:23) _____

    Is not that / that man that son of David?

© 1999 BJU Press. Reproduction prohibited.

Match the following phrases with their meanings. These common English phrases contain Latin pronouns. Note that the macrons are omitted. In most of the translations, prepositions have been supplied to make the meaning of the phrase clear. How and why we supply these prepositions will become clear in later chapters. In number 6 the phrase *quomodo* has become one word in English.

D 1. hoc loco	A.	He who teaches learns.
B 2. hoc tempore	B.	at this time
H 3. hoc mense	C.	in what manner, how
I 4. hoc titule	D.	in this place
G 5. hoc sensu	E.	what for what, something in return for something
C 6. quomodo	F.	What I have written I have written.
A 7. qui docet discit	G.	in this sense
E 8. quid pro quo	H.	in this month
J 9. quid times	I.	with this title
F 10. quod scripsi scripsi	J.	What do you fear?

Activity G

Write each phrase in Latin. Working with participles provides a review of vocabulary words you have worked with. If necessary, you may look up the words in the Vocābulārium, first in the English-to-Latin section and then in the Latin-to-English section to find the principal parts or other needed information.

1. the men walking on the road (subject) _____

   virī/hominēs in viā ambulantēs

2. the boys running in the forest (direct object) _____

   puerōs currentēs in silvā

3. the mothers calling daughters (subject) _____

   mātrēs vocantēs fīliās

4. the children having been found (indirect object) _____

   līberīs inventīs

5. the lives having been saved (direct object) _____

   vītās servātās

© 1999 BJU Press. Reproduction prohibited.

Translate these sentences, which are taken from verses in the Vulgate and Beza's translation of the book of Acts. Do not refer to your Bible while you are doing this activity. Use obvious English derivatives to determine the meanings of new words not defined for you.

Remember that Latin word order can vary more than English word order. For example, a participle may precede the noun it modifies or it may be separated from the noun it modifies by one or more words. In number 3 the participle is a predicate adjective that modifies the pronoun that is the understood subject of the verb. In number 8 the word order has been changed slightly and two words have been supplied to make the translation easier. The shortened form *lapidārunt* has been replaced with the complete word form *lapidāvērunt*.

When four periods are placed at the end of a quotation, the remainder of the sentence has been omitted.

1. Exsurgēns° Petrus in mediō° frātrum dīxit. . . . (V 1:15) _____

   Peter, rising (up) in the midst of the brothers, said/spoke. . . .
   _____

   [°rise up; °the middle, midst]

2. Stāns autem Petrus cum undecim levāvit° vocem° suam [and spoke] eīs. . . . (V 2:14)

   However/Moreover Peter, standing with the eleven, lifted up his voice [and spoke] to them. . . .

   (Without context, students have no basis for choosing between *however*

   [°lifted up; °voice] **and *moreover.*)**

3. Erant autem persevērantes in doctrinā apostolōrum. (V 2:42) _____

   Moreover/However they were persevering in the doctrine of the apostles.

4. Et exsiliēns° stetit et ambulābat et intrāvit° cum illīs in templum, ambulāns et exiliēns

   et laudāns° Dominum. (V 3:8) ___ *And leaping up he stood and walked and entered with*

   them/those into the temple, walking and leaping and praising the Lord.

   [°leap up; °enter; °praise]

5. Tunc° Petrus replētus° Spiritū Sanctō dīxit eīs. . . . (B 4:8) _____

   Then Peter filled / having been filled with the Holy Spirit, said to them. . . .

   [°then; °fill, make full]

6. Petrus autem et Joannes respondentēs dīxērunt eīs. . . . (B 4:19) _____

   However/Moreover Peter and John, responding, said to them. . . .

7. Ecce, conspiciō° coelōs° apertōs°, et Fīlium illum hominis adstantem° ad dextram°

   Deī. (B 7:56) ___ *Behold I see the heavens (having been) opened,*

   and that Son of man standing at the right hand of God.

   [°perceive, see; °heaven; °open; °stand, stand by; °the right hand]

8. Et eum [*illum virum*] ejectum° extra° urbem, lapidāvērunt°. (B 7:58) _____

   And they threw stones at him [that man] having been cast outside the city.

   [°having been cast out; °outside; °they threw stones at, they stoned]

© 1999 BJU Press. Reproduction prohibited.

Activity I

Translate each ablative absolute phrase literally. If the phrase does not contain a participle, supply the English participle *being*.

1. librō scriptō ___ *the book having been written* ___

2. librō novō ___ *the book being new* ___

3. consiliīs factīs ___ *the plans having been made* ___

4. verbō dictō ___ *the word having been spoken* ___

5. Hannibale victō ___ *Hannibal having been conquered* ___

6. Cincinnātō duce ___ *Cincinnatus being the general/leader* ___

7. Cincinnātō in agrō labōrante ___ *Cincinnatus working in the field* ___

8. diē brevī ___ *the day being short* ___

Activity J

Translate each sentence literally. Then in the second blank, translate the ablative absolute freely. If the ablative absolute contains no participle, supply the word *being* in the literal translation.

1. Omnibus territīs, virī ex urbe curcurrērunt.

   ___ *All having been terrified, the men ran from the city.* ___

   ___ *Because/When all were terrified* ___

2. Caesāre terram tenente, multī servī° ad Rōmam missī sunt.

   ___ *Caesar holding the land, many slaves were sent to Rome.* ___

   ___ *Because/When Caesar was holding / held the land* ___

   [°slaves]

3. Hīs rēbus factīs, mīlitēs ad Rōman venērunt.

   ___ *These things having been done, the soldiers came to Rome.* ___

   ___ *Because/When these things were done* ___

4. Verbīs audītīs, dux imperium dedit.

   ___ *The words having been heard, the leader gave a command.* ___

   ___ *When he heard the words / When the words were heard* ___

5. Bellō longō, mīlitēs fīnem pugnae° illīus voluērunt°.

   ___ *The war being long, the soldiers wanted the/an end of that battle.* ___

   ___ *Because/Since the war was long* ___

   [°battle; °wanted]

© 1999 BJU Press. Reproduction prohibited.

Activity K

Write the letter for the literal or basic meaning of each derivative. After the derivative write the first principal part of the Latin source word. The derivative preceded by an asterisk has a prefix before the root from which the derivative has come.

D 1. *adjacent _____jaceō_____   A. sitting

J 2. agent _____agō_____   B. rising again

F 3. ambulance _____ambulō_____   C. running

I 4. cadence _____cadō_____   D. lying near

E 5. credence _____crēdō_____   E. believing

C 6. current _____currō_____   F. walking

B 7. resurgent _____resurgō_____   G. knowing

G 8. science _____sciō_____   H. conquering

A 9. sedentary _____sedeō_____   I. falling

H 10. Vincent _____vincō_____   J. acting, doing

Activity L

Keep building your English vocabulary as you add to your Latin vocabulary. In this activity you are to give the Latin verb from which the derivative came. Give the principal parts of each verb. Even if the Latin verb is unfamiliar to you, make a reasonable guess. In number 6, the letter *j* replaces the letter *i* in the Latin source word.

1. *appellation* from _____appellō (1)_____

2. *creation* from _____creō (1)_____

3. *correction* from _____corrigō, -ere, -rexī, -rectus_____

4. *possession* from _____possideō, -ēre, -sēdī, -sessus_____

5. *education* from _____ē + ducō, -ere, duxī, ductus / ēdūcō_____

6. *ejection* from _____ē + iaciō, -ere, iēcī, iactus / ēiciō_____

7. *laudation/laudatory/laud* from _____laudō (1)_____

© 1999 BJU Press. Reproduction prohibited.

This activity has a dual purpose: (1) to review vocabulary words in this chapter and (2) to increase your English vocabulary. In each blank write the Latin word from which the underlined English word came directly or indirectly. Also write the information that is given in the vocabulary listing of each word. When necessary, check the vocabulary lists in this chapter and be sure to learn any words you must check.

1. The planets Jupiter, Venus, and Mars are <u>celestial</u> bodies named for three Roman deities. _____ *coelum, -ī, n., heaven, sky* _____

2. Susan is taking <u>vocal</u> lessons and will sing a solo in church on Sunday.
_____ *vōx, vōcis, f., voice* _____

3. There is no <u>aperture</u> in that wall; so the men climbed over it.
_____ *aperiō, -īre, -uī, -pertus, -a, -um, to open* _____

4. Scientists study the <u>motion</u> of the stars.
_____ *moveō, -ēre, mōvī, mōtus, -a, -um, to move* _____

5. The library shelves are <u>replete</u> with good books.
_____ *repleō, -ēre, -ēvī, -tus, -a, -um, to fill / to make full* _____

6. The <u>gubernatorial</u> election was won by the man best qualified to be governor of our state. _____ *gūbernātiō, -ōnis, f., government* _____

7. The purpose of the court system is to prevent <u>injustices</u>.
_____ *iniustitia, -ae, f., injustice* _____

8. <u>Avarice</u> is the opposite of generosity.
_____ *avārārus, -a, -um, greedy* _____

9. Each week our newspaper publishes the <u>obituaries</u> of people who have died.
_____ *obeō, -īre, -īvī, -ītus, -a, -um, to go away / to die* _____

10. The students and faculty of that college will soon hold the <u>tricentennial</u> celebration of their school. _____ *trecentī, three hundred* _____

© 1999 BJU Press. Reproduction prohibited.

CAPITULUM XXII

© 1999 BJU Press. Reproduction prohibited.

Activity A

Answer each question in Latin. The questions require thought, and not all of them can be answered by quoting from the paragraphs. Your answers may be brief. Be careful to use inflections that would be correct if your answers were in complete sentences.

If necessary, you may check the list of new words.

1. In cuius exercitū multī pauperēs Rōmānī conscriptī sunt? _____

   Mariī/Marī / in exercitū Mariī/Marī

2. Eratne stipendium militum in exercitū Marī agrī et pecūnia? _____

   Erat / Ita vērē erat agrī et pecūnia.

3. Erat exercitus Marī fidēlis ducī aut fidēlis Rōmae? _____

   Erat fidēlis ducī/Mariō.

4. Contrā quem ducem Marius primum bellum civile pugnāvit? _____

   Contrā Sullam pugnāvit.

5. Qui erant ducēs in Prīmō Triumvirātū? _____

   Pompeius Magnus, Iulius Caesar, et Crassus Dīvēs

6. Cuius exercitus Galliam vīcit? _____

   Exercitus Iuliī/Iulī Caesaris Galliam vīcit.

7. Qui Caesarem venīre ad Rōmam sine exercitū eius iussit? _____

   Senātus Rōmānus

8. Quod flūmen Caesar cum exercitū transit? _____

   Rubicōnem flūmen transit.

9. Ubi Pompeius et senātōrēs exercitum contrā Caesarem conscripsērunt? _____

   in Graeciā

10. Ubi Pompeius necātus est? _____

    in Aegyptō

Match the terms in column 2 with the proper nouns in column 1.

_____F_____ 1. Sulla

_____A_____ 2. Crassus

_____B_____ 3. Iulius Caesar

_____G_____ 4. Pompeius Magnus

_____D_____ 5. Rubicon

_____E_____ 6. Aegyptus

_____C_____ 7. Marius

A. a very rich man

B. conqueror of Gallia

C. general who enlisted many poor men

D. river that Caesar crossed

E. place where Pompey died

F. enemy of Marius

G. friend and later an enemy of Caesar

Activity C

Write each phrase in Latin. Be sure that each adjective agrees in gender, number, and case with the noun that it modifies. An adjective may or may not be in the same declension as the noun it modifies.

1. a shorter time (nominative) _____ *tempus brevius* _____

2. a very brave man (dative) _____ *virō audācissimō* _____

3. a stronger soldier (dative) _____ *militī fortiōrī* _____

4. a rather sad boy (accusative) _____ *puerum tristiōrem* _____

5. a longer road (ablative) _____ *viā longiōre* _____

6. of the bravest general (genitive) _____ *ducis fortissimī* _____

7. longer wars (accusative) _____ *bella longiōra* _____

8. of braver soldiers (genitive) _____ *mīlitum fortiōrum* _____

© 1999 BJU Press. Reproduction prohibited.

© 1999 BJU Press. Reproduction prohibited.

Activity D

Translate each sentence.

1. Vīta Cicerōnis erat longior quam vīta Iuliī Caesaris. _____
   The life of Cicero / Cicero's life was longer than the life of Julius Caesar / Julius Caesar's life.

2. Vīta Iuliī Caesaris erat brevior quam vīta Pompeiī Magnī. _____
   The life of Julius Caesar / Julius Caesar's life was shorter than the life of Pompey the Great.

3. Inter trēs virōs in Prīmō Triumvirātū, Caesar brevissimam vītam habuit. _____
   Among the three men in the First Triumvirate, Caesar had the shortest life.

4. Caesar erat dux parātissimus in bellīs Gallicīs. _____ *Caesar was a very well prepared*
   _____ *general in the Gallic wars.* (Good English grammar requires the word *well*
   before a participle used as an adjective in phrases such as *very well prepared*.)

5. Mīlitēs Caesaris erant quam fortissimī in proeliīs. _____
   Caesar's soldiers were as brave as possible in battles.

6. Tempus sine bellīs in Rōmā erat brevior. _____
   The time without wars in Rome was rather brief.

Activity E

Write each sentence in English.

1. Publius erat amīcus fidēllimus. _____
   Publius was a very faithful friend.

2. Decem puerī currēbant. Quintus erat celerrimus. _____
   Ten boys were running. Quintus was the fastest.

3. Hic liber est facilior quam ille liber. _____
   This book is easier than that book.

4. Vulnus° est acerrimum. _____
   The wound is very painful.

   [°wound]

5. Rōma et Carthāgō bella tria pugnābant. Secundum bellum erat longissimum. _____
   Rome and Carthage fought three wars. The second war was the longest.

6. Exercitus Rōmānus erat quam parātissimus. _____
   The Roman army was as prepared as possible.

Activity F

Write each sentence in Latin.

1. My book is shorter than your book. _____

    _____ *Liber meus est brevior quam liber tuus.* _____

2. This book is very similar to my book. _____

    _____ *Hic liber est simillimus librō meō.* _____

3. That book is as new as possible. _____

    _____ *Ille liber est quam novissimus.* _____

4. The story in my book is rather sad. _____

    _____ *Fābula in librō meō est tristior.* _____

5. The story tells about very poor families. _____

    _____ *Fabula dē familiīs pauperrimīs narrat.* _____

Activity G

Write each sentence in English. When an adjective has no noun to modify, supply the words *thing(s)* or *men/people* to indicate the understood noun in the Latin sentence.

These sentences are quotations or revisions of statements found in Latin literature. Meanings are not given for new words if English derivatives suggest the obvious meanings.

1. Bona facile mutantur in° peiora. (Quintilian) _____

    _____ *Good things are easily changed into worse things.* _____

    [°into]

2. Saepe īra dē levissimīs causīs existit°. (Culman) _____

    _____ *Often anger arises from very light causes.* _____

    [°arise]

3. Vir quī contentus est maximās et certissimās° divitiās° habet. (Publilius Syrus)

    _____

    A man who is content has the greatest / very great and most certain / very certain riches.

    [°most certain; °riches]

4. Dīligentia durissima vincit. (Culman) *Diligence conquers the hardest / very hard things.*

    _____ *(A possible but not good translation: Very hard diligence conquers.)* _____

5. Experientia est magister optimus in rēbus omnibus. (Publilius Syrus) _____

    _____ *Experience is the best teacher in all things.* _____

© 1999 BJU Press. Reproduction prohibited.

These sentences are *based on* verses in Beza's translation of the New Testament. Write each sentence in English. Only the portions in quotation marks come directly from the Bible. Latin portions not in quotation marks and bracketed portions are paraphrases or explanations of portions too difficult for you to translate now.

You need not copy long passages of English.

1. Vir appellātus Joānnēs dē Christō dīxit, "prior mē erat." (John 1:15) _____

   A man named John spoke/said concerning Christ, "he was before me."

2. Christus erat major quam Joānnēs. (John 1:27) _____

   Christ was greater than John.

3. Jēsus dē Joānne Baptistā dīxit, "[the person that is] minimus in regnō est major [than John]." (Luke 7:28) _____ *Jesus said concerning John the Baptist,*

   "[the person that is] least in the kingdom is greater [than John]."

4. [A grain of mustard seed] "minimum est omnium seminum° quae in terra sunt." (Mark 4:31) _____

   [A grain of mustard seed] "is the smallest/least of all the seeds which are on/in the earth."

   [°seed]

5. [The Pharisees asked Pilate to set a guard at Jesus' tomb so that the disciples could not steal His body and say that He arose. They said that] "ultimus error" [would be] "peior/pejor" [than the first]. (Matthew 27:64) _____

   [They said that] "the last error" [would be] "worse" [than the first].

6. [The disciples asked Jesus, "Who] maximus est in regnō coelōrum?" (Matthew 18:1)

   _____

   [The disciples asked Jesus, "Who] is the greatest in the kingdom of the heavens?"

7. "Sed majorem offert° gratiam." (James 4:6) _____

   "But he offers/presents more/greater grace."

   [°offer, present]

© 1999 BJU Press. Reproduction prohibited.

Activity I

Translate each sentence into Latin. Check pages 325-26 for correct comparative forms.

1. Marcus was with a rather faithful friend. _____

    Marcus erat cum amicō fidēliōre.

    _____

2. The Gracchi brothers were friends of the rather poor Romans. _____

    Gracchī frātrēs erant amīcī Rōmānōrum pauperiōrum.

    _____

3. The wars against Carthage were longer than the war against Britain. _____

    Bella contrā Carthāginem erant longiōra quam bellum contrā Britānniam.

    _____

4. The better plans of Cicero saved Rome from bad plans of a very bad man. _____

    Consilia meliōra Cicerōnis Rōmam ab consiliīs malīs virī pessimī servāvērunt/servābant.

    _____

Activity J

Translate each English sentence into a Latin sentence.

1. The days in winter are shorter than the days in summer. _____

    Diēs in hieme sunt breviōrēs quam diēs in aetāte.

2. My horse is swifter than your horse. _____

    Equus meus est celerior quam equus tuus.

3. Caesar's soldiers were as brave as possible. _____

    Mīlitēs Caesaris erant quam fortissimī.

4. The gods of the Romans were very similar to the gods of the Greeks. _____

    Deī Rōmānōrum erant simillimī deīs Graecōrum.

5. The city of Rome is very large. _____

    Urbs Rōmae est maxima.

6. Many soldiers in Marius's army were rather poor. _____

    Multī mīlitēs in exercitū Mariī/Marī erant pauperiōrēs.

© 1999 BJU Press. Reproduction prohibited.

Activity K

Complete each comparison by writing the English word that comes from the stem of the Latin word. To spell the English word, follow the pattern of derivation that is shown in the first pair of words.

1. orātiōnis : oration :: mūtātiōnis : _____ *mutation*

2. resurrectiōnis : resurrection :: cognitiōnis : _____ *cognition*

3. dominātiōnis : domination :: investigātiōnis : _____ *investigation*

4. appellātus : appellation :: terminātus : _____ *termination*

5. conscriptus : conscription :: coniunctus : _____ *conjunction*

6. audācis : audacity :: brevis : _____ *brevity*

7. fidēlis : fidelity :: facilis : _____ *facility*

8. cīvilis : civility :: celer : _____ *celerity*

9. longus : longitude :: magnus : _____ *magnitude*

10. multus : multitude :: fortis : _____ *fortitude*

Activity L

This activity is based on the three degrees of irregular adjectives. Match the meanings with the loan words and loan phrases.

___D___ 1. bonus

___F___ 2. bona fide

___C___ 3. magnum opus

___E___ 4. optimum

___H___ 5. maximum

___A___ 6. minimum

___B___ 7. major

___G___ 8. minor

A. the smallest possible amount or degree

B. greater than others

C. a great work, literary or artistic

D. something beyond what is expected

E. the best condition

F. in good faith

G. lesser in importance

H. the greatest possible amount or degree

© 1999 BJU Press. Reproduction prohibited.

Activity M

The words in column 1 are derivatives from irregular Latin adjectives. Match the meanings with the derivatives.

_C_ 1. ameliorate	A.	a rating before others in the same class
_E_ 2. pejorate	B.	one who expects the worst outcome
_A_ 3. priority	C.	to make better
_D_ 4. superiority	D.	a rating above others in the same class
_F_ 5. optimist	E.	to make worse
_B_ 6. pessimist	F.	one who expects the best outcome

Activity N

Match each derivative with the meaning based on its Latin origin.

_C_ 1. alien	A.	the right to choose what one desires
_E_ 2. motion	B.	choice of a governor
_K_ 3. avaricious	C.	a person from another country
_L_ 4. obituary	D.	a name
_D_ 5. appellation	E.	the act or process of moving
_H_ 6. education	F.	involving hard work
_A_ 7. option	G.	a hereditary physical change
_G_ 8. mutation	H.	the act of leading forth or bringing up
_F_ 9. laborious	I.	the act of making right
_B_ 10. gubernatorial election	J.	the quality of being unfair; a wrong
_I_ 11. correction	K.	having a great desire to gain wealth; greedy
_J_ 12. injustice	L.	a brief biography of one who has died

© 1999 BJU Press. Reproduction prohibited.

CAPITULUM XXIII

© 1999 BJU Press. Reproduction prohibited.

Activity A

Answer each question in Latin. Not all your answers need to be complete sentences.

1. Ubi Marcus Antōnius partem exercitūs Caesaris ducēbat? _____

    in Ītaliā

    Where did Mark Antony lead part of Caesar's army?

2. Erat Marcus Antōnius dux bonus? _____ *Ita vērē / Erat dux bonus.* _____

    Was Mark Antony a good general?

3. Quis ōrātiōnēs dē vitiīs Marcī Antōnī faciēbat? _____

    Cicerō (ōrātiōnēs dē vitiīs Marcī Antōnī faciēbat).

    Who made speeches about the faults of Mark Antony?

4. Cūr Marcus Antōnius inimīcitiam ad Cicerōnem habēbat? _____

    (Quod) Cicerō ōrātiōnēs dē vitiīs Marcī Antōnī / eius faciēbat.

    Why did Mark Antony have enmity toward Cicero?

5. Quis Iulium Caesarem dictātōrem fēcit? _____

    Iulius Caesar / Ipse

    Who made Julius Caesar dictator?

6. Quī Iulium Caesarem necāvērunt? _____

    senātōrēs quī erant inimīcī Iuliī/Iulī Caesaris

    Who killed Julius Caesar?

7. Erant virī in Secundō Triumvirītū amīcī? _____

    Nōn erant. / Nōn amīcī erant. / Minimē.

    Were the men in the Second Triumvirate friends?

8. Quis nōmen Cicerōnis in tabulā° inimīcōrum habēbat? _____

    Marcus Antōnius (nōmen Cicerōnis in tabulā inimīcōrum habēbat).

    [°tablet] **Who had the name of Cicero on/in a table/list of enemies?**

9. Quī duo ducēs in ultimō bellō cīvilī pugnābant? _____

    Marcus Antōnius et Octāvius Caesar

    What two generals fought in the last civil war?

Written exercises
189

10. In quō modō° Marcus Antōnius obīvit? _____

_____
Sē necāvit.

[°means, manner] **In what manner did Mark Antony die?**

11. Quid Octāvius Caesar constituit? _____

_____
Imperium Rōmānum (constituit).

What did Octavius Caesar establish?

Activity B

Each Latin word or phrase is found in "Secundus Triumvirātus." Write the letter for each grammatical term with the matching Latin word or phrase.

_____E_____ 1. contrā Pompeium   A. direct object

_____B_____ 2. dux bonus   B. predicate noun

_____A_____ 3. multa vitia   C. adverb

_____J_____ 4. dictātōrem   D. object of a preposition

_____F_____ 5. manentibus   E. prepositional phrase

_____H_____ 6. sēnātōrēs   F. present participle

_____D_____ 7. tabulā   G. ablative absolute

_____C_____ 8. mox   H. subject

_____I_____ 9. reī publicae Rōmānae   I. phrase in the genitive case

_____G_____ 10. victōriā perfectā   J. objective complement

© 1999 BJU Press. Reproduction prohibited.

In Part 1, translate each phrase into English. In Part 2, translate each phrase into Latin.

Part 1

1. dux pugnāns in Hispāniā (subject) _____

   the general fighting in Spain

2. Cicerōnem ōrātiōnem facientem (direct object) _____

   Cicero making a speech

3. Caesar ā senātōribus necātus (subject) _____

   Caesar (having been) killed by senators

4. trēs virī sē coniunctūrī in Secundō Triumvirātō (subject) _____

   three men about to / going to join themselves in the Second Triumvirate

5. inimīcōs necandōs (direct object) _____

   enemies (necessary) to be killed

Part 2

1. the Romans having many gods (subject) _____

   Rōmānī multōs deōs habentēs

2. the Romans about to praise their gods (subject) _____

   Rōmānī deōs suōs laudātūrī

3. the names of the many gods having been taught to boys and girls (subject) _____

   nōmina multōrum deōrum puerīs et puellīs docta

4. stories written about Roman gods (direct object) _____

   fabulās dē deīs Rōmānīs scriptās

5. the stories about the Roman gods not to be believed (direct object) _____

   fabulās dē deīs Rōmānīs nōn credendās

© 1999 BJU Press. Reproduction prohibited.

Translate each sentence. In number 5, the word *futūrās* may be translated "future" because the Romans themselves made this participle a regular adjective. Two sentences contain ablative absolutes. In Chapter 21 you were shown several different ways to translate these. You may translate them either literally (using just the meanings of the Latin participles) or by using one of the ways you were shown.

1. Pecūnia crescēns virōs ad cūram crescentem dūcit. _____

   Increasing money leads men to increasing concern/care.

2. Īra nostra est vincenda. _____

   Our anger is (necessary) to be conquered / must be conquered.

3. Īrā victā, puer est fīlius melior. _____

   Anger having been conquered / When he has conquered his anger, the/a boy is a better son.

4. Illa puella īram eius victūra est. _____

   That girl is going to conquer her anger.

5. Rēs futūrās nōn scīmus. _____

   We do not know the things going to be / future things.

6. Multī librī sunt legendī. _____

   Many books are (necessary) to be read / must be read.

7. In scholā nōs multōs librōs lectūrī sumus. _____

   In school we are going to read many books.

8. Illa patria ā Rōmā victa imperium Rōmānum crēvit. _____

   That country (having been) conquered by Rome increased the Roman empire.

9. Senātor Rōmānus dīxit, "Carthāgō dēlenda est." _____

   A/The Roman senator said, "Carthage is (necessary) to be destroyed / must be destroyed."

10. Asiā victā, dux Rōmānus servōs° multōs in Ītaliam mīsit. (Pliny the Elder)

    Asia having been conquered / When Asia had been conquered,

    the Roman general/leader sent many slaves into Italy.

    [°slaves]

© 1999 BJU Press. Reproduction prohibited.

Translate each sentence. In these sentences *fabula* means "myth." In number 5, *orientem sōlis* means "rising of the sun, the east" and *occidentem sōlis* means "setting of the sun, the west."

1. Apollo erat geminus Dianae. In Graeciā et in Rōmā erat deus sōlis° et lūcis.

   Apollo was the twin of Diana.

   In Greece and in Rome he was the god of the sun and of light.

   [°sun]

2. Apollo erat Graecus deus. Quoque ā Rōmānīs Apollo appellātus est.

   Apollo was a Greek god.

   He was called/named Apollo also by the Romans.

3. Diana ā Graecīs Artemis appellābātur. _____

   Diana was called Artemis by the Greeks.

4. Multae fabulae dē Apolline et Dianā narrātae sunt. _____

   Many stories/myths have been told about Apollo and Diana.

5. In fabulīs Apollo carrum in caelō omnī° diē° ab orientem sōlis ad occidentem sōlis

   agēbat°. _____

   In myths Apollo drove a chariot in the sky every day from the east to the west.

   [°every; °day; °drove]

6. Diana erat dea lūnae°. Quoque carrō trāns caelum vēnit. Ex librīs fabulārum discere

   dē eā potes. _____ *Diana was the goddess of the moon. She also came across the sky*

   by / with / by means of a chariot. From books of myths you are able to learn about her.

   [°moon]

7. Virī et fēminae in urbe clāmābant, "Magna est Diana Ephesiōrum!" (Acts 19:34)

   Men and women in the city were shouting, "Great is Diana of the Ephesians!"

8. Multī virī Dianae templa faciēbant. Illī virī sine deā Dianā nōn esse optābant.

   (Acts 19:23-29) _____ *Many men were making / made temples for Diana.*

   Those men did not want/choose to be without the goddess Diana.

9. Apollo et Diana in imāginātiōne virōrum et fēminārum et in fabulīs sōlum°

   vivēbant. _____

   Apollo and Diana lived only in the imagination of men and women and in myths.

   [°only]

© 1999 BJU Press. Reproduction prohibited.

Before each term, write *abl.*, *acc.*, or *loc.* to indicate which case is used to express the idea indicated. Then write *yes* if a preposition should be used and *no* if no preposition should be used.

loc.—no	1. place where, the name of a city
abl.—yes	2. place where, not the name of a city or the word *domus*
loc.—no	3. place where, the noun *domus*
abl.—yes	4. place from which
abl.—no	5. place from which, name of a city
acc.—no	6. place to which, name of a city
abl.—no	7. time when
abl.—no	8. time within which
acc.—no	9. time how long
abl.—yes	10. ablative of agent
abl.—no	11. ablative of means

Translate each phrase.

1. within an hour _____ *hōrā* _____
2. in the forest _____ *in silvā* _____
3. for ten days _____ *decem diēs* _____
4. at home _____ *domī* _____
5. book (having been) read by the girls _____ *liber lectus ā/ab puellīs* _____
6. book (having been) written with a stylus _____ *liber scriptus stilō* _____
7. away from Europe _____ *ab Eurōpā* _____
8. to Troy _____ *Trōiam* _____

© 1999 BJU Press. Reproduction prohibited.

Translate sentences 1-6 into English and 7-11 into Latin. Give special attention to expressions of place and time, which are found in some of the sentences.

1. Mars erat Rōmā deus bellī. Multa templa in honōre eius in Ītaliā aedificāta sunt.

   Mars was the god of war at/in Rome.

   Many temples were built in his honor in Italy.

2. Prīmō Mars erat deus Rōmānus agrōrum et gregum. Multae fabulae dē° Marte ab fabulīs Graecīs dē deō Āre° vēnērunt. *At first Mars was the Roman god of fields and (of) flocks. Many myths about Mars came from Greek myths about the god Ares.*

   [°concerning; °Ares, -is, Greek god of war]

3. In fabulīs Rōmānīs Mars erat pater Rōmulī. *In Roman myths Mars was the father of Romulus.*

4. Honor Martī° mense° Martiī° datum est. *Honor was given to Mars in the month of March.*

   [°Mars; °month; °of March]

5. Post victōriās mīlitēs Rōmam redēbant° et victōriās celebrābant. Martem laudābant.

   After victories, soldiers returned to Rome and celebrated the victories.

   They praised Mars.

   [°return]

6. Rōmānī multās diēs victōriam celebrābant. *The Romans celebrated a/the victory (for) many days.*

7. That man was a general in the Roman republic. *Ille vir / Vir ille erat dux/imperātor in rē publicā Rōmānā.*

8. He lived in Rome. *Rōmā vivēbat.*

9. After a great victory he returned to Rome. *Post magnam victōriam Rōmam redēbat.*

10. Within one year he led his army to Spain. *Ūnō annō ad Hispāniam exercitum suum dūxit.*

11. In Spain he fought the third battle. *In Hispāniā proelium tertium pugnābat/pugnāvit.*

© 1999 BJU Press. Reproduction prohibited.

Translate each sentence. Give special attention to expressions of place and time.

1. Antīquīs temporibus Rōmānī Mecurium adōrābant. Nōmen Graecum deī illīus erat
   Hermes. _____*In ancient times the Romans worshiped Mercury.*_____
   _____*The Greek name of that god was Hermes.*_____

2. Mercurius erat frāter Apollinis et fīlius Iovis°. Multa saecula° hic deus ā Rōmānīs
   adōrātus est. _____*Mercury was the brother of Apollo and the son of Jupiter.*_____
   _____*For many centuries this god was worshiped by the Romans.*_____
   [°genitive form of *Iuppiter;* °centuries]

3. Mercurius erat deus viātorum° et mercātōrum°. Quoque erat fūr° et fraudātor°. Breve
   tempus frātrem eius fraudābat°. _____*Mercury was the god of travelers and of merchants.*_____
   _____*Also he was a thief and a deceiver. For a brief time he deceived his brother.*_____
   [°of travelers; °of merchants; °thief; °deceiver; °deceive]

4. Mercurius soleās° habentēs ālās° gerēbat°. Nuntiōs° longa spatia° ab Iove
   transportābat°. _____*Mercury wore sandals having wings.*_____
   _____*He carried messages long distances from Jupiter / from Jupiter long distances.*_____
   [°sandal; °wing; °wear; °message; °distance; °carry]

5. In fabulīs Graecīs, brevī tempore post mortem mortālis,° Hermes animam mortālis
   illīus ad habitātiōnem° mortuōrum° transportāvit. _____*In Greek myths, (within) a short time after*_____
   _____*the death of a mortal, Hermes carried the soul of that mortal to the abode of the dead / dead people.*_____
   [°a person, a mortal; °abode, habitation; °of the dead (people)]

Translate these phrases into English, supplying prepositions where they are needed.

1. fabula lecta ā puerō _____*(the/a) myth/story read by the/a boy*_____
2. deus portātus carrō _____*the/a god carried by a chariot*_____
3. deī adōrātī Rōmā _____*gods/deities worshiped at/in Rome*_____
4. fabulae dē deīs _____*myths about/concerning gods/deities*_____
5. virī venientēs Rōmam _____*men coming to Rome*_____
6. deī et deae illīs temporibus _____*gods and goddesses in/at those times*_____
7. liber lectus octō hōrīs _____*the/a book read within eight hours*_____
8. puella legēns octō hōrās _____*the/a girl reading (for) eight hours*_____
9. vir ambulāns quinque milia passuum° _____*the/a man walking five miles*_____
   [°a mile]

© 1999 BJU Press. Reproduction prohibited.

© 1999 BJU Press. Reproduction prohibited.

Activity J

Answer each question on the basis of Greek and Roman mythology. The questions may contain relative pronouns, interrogative pronouns, or interrogative adjectives. These are compared in Chapter 20.

1. Quis erat deus Rōmānus quī animās mortuōrum ad habitātiōnem mortuōrum

   transportābat? _____ *Mercurius/Mercury*

2. Quid erat nōmen deī Graecī qui erat Mercuriō similis? _____ *Hermes*

3. Quid erat nōmen deae Graecae qui erat Dianae similis? _____ *Artemis*

4. Quī deus Rōmānus erat deus sōlis? _____ *Apollo*

5. Quae dea Rōmāna erat dea lūnae? _____ *Diana*

6. Quī deus Rōmānus erat deus habitātiōnis mortuōrum? _____ *Pluto*

7. Quī deus Rōmānus erat deus coelī? _____ *Iuppiter/Jupiter*

8. Quid est nōmen Graecum habitātiōnis mortuōrum? _____ *Hades*

9. Quī deus Rōmānus soleās habentēs alās habēbat? _____ *Mercurius/Mercury*

10. Quī deus Rōmānus erat frāter Mercurī? _____ *Apollo*

Activity K

Write the Latin prefix and the root from which each word is made. Choose the second or the fourth principal part of the verb. If you cannot recall the Latin verb for the English meaning indicated by the definition, look for it in the English-to-Latin section of the Vocābulārium. Then, if necessary, look for the spelling of the stems in the Latin-to-English section.

Notice that in each definition the meanings of the two parts are in reverse order: verb meaning then the prefix meaning. The meanings given are literal; consequently, they do not all read smoothly as do dictionary definitions. The purpose is to help you understand the basic meanings of these English derivatives.

1. decadent, "falling down" _____ *dē cadere*

2. exclamation, "(something that is) shouted out" _____ *ex clāmātus*

3. excursion, "(a trip) running out from a certain place" _____ *ex cursus*

4. edict, "(a formal statement) spoken out" _____ *ē dictus*

5. describe, "to write about" _____ *dē scrībere*

6. effected, "(accomplished) done out" _____ *ex factus*

7. affected, "(influenced) done to" _____ *ad factus*

8. elected, "chosen out" _____ *ē lectus*

9. deducted, "(taken from) led down from" _____ *dē ductus*

10. demoted, "moved down" _____ *dē mōtus*

Written exercises   **197**

Activity L

Before each English derivative, write the matching letter that shows the Latin origin of the present English word and the present meaning of the word or a word in the phrase.

D 1. edifice	A.	legō, -ere, lēgī, lectus, to choose
I 2. "Ave Maria"	B.	pugnō (1), to fight
G 3. canticle	C.	corrigō, -ere, -rexī, -rectus, to correct
F 4. cogitation	D.	aedificiō (1), to build
C 5. corrigible	E.	maneō, -ēre, mansī, mansus, -a, -um, to remain
B 6. pugnacious	F.	cōgitō (1), to think
H 7. disciple	G.	cantō (1), to sing
J 8. fugitive	H.	discō, -ere, didicī, to learn
A 9. elect	I.	aveō, -ēre, to be well, hail!
E 10. mansion	J.	fugiō, -ere, fūgī, fūgitus, -a, -um, to flee

Activity M

From the list of new words on page 334, give the Latin word and its meaning from which the English derivative came, directly or indirectly.

1. consent ___*consentiō—to agree*___

2. constitution ___*constituō—to found, establish*___

3. perfection ___*perficiō—to accomplish, complete*___

4. oratorical ___*ōrātor—orator*___

5. ultimatum ___*ultimus—last*___

6. inimical ___*inimīcitia—hatred, hostility*___

© 1999 BJU Press. Reproduction prohibited.